*The World's Most Accurate*

# ANTIQUES, COLLECTIBLES
### AND OTHER TREASURES
# PRICE GUIDE

*Companion Publication for*

## DIRECTORY OF BUYERS

Compiled by
**TONY AND MARILEE HYMAN**

Written by
**TRASH OR TREASURE LISTEES**

**TREASURE HUNT PUBLICATIONS**
Shell Beach, California

**Where to Sell Series of books by Tony Hyman**
>    1980 The Where To Sell Anything and Everything Book (1st ed.)
>    1984 Where To Sell Anything and Everything by Mail (2nd ed.)
>    1986 Cash For Your Undiscovered Treasures (3rd ed.)
>    1989 I'll Buy That! (4th ed.)
>    1992 I'll Buy That Too! (5th ed.)
>    1993 Where to Sell It (6th ed.)
>    1994 Trash or Treasure (7th ed.)
>    1994 World's Most Accurate Price Guide
>    1997 Trash or Treasure Directory of Buyers 1997-98 (8th ed.)

**Books on tobacco collectibles by Tony Hyman**
>    1989 The World of Smoking and Tobacco at Auction
>    1979 Handbook of American Cigar Boxes

Treasure Hunt Publications
PO Box 3028
Shell Beach, CA 93448


Designer: Steve Gussman, North Hollywood

PRINTING: 0 9 8 7 6                    ISBN: 0-937111-08-2

Dear Reader:

Welcome to *The World's Most Accurate Price Guide*. That's quite a claim! Can we prove it? We sure can!

To find out why this price guide is different and more accurate let's start by taking a look at other general price guides on the market and how they are put together. Most price guide "values" are derived as a composite of auction results, prices being asked in shops, prices being asked in ads appearing in antiques publications, what antique dealers claim they got for an item and what collectors claim they paid for an item. Clerks type these figures into a computer which averages them. These averages are published as the "value." That's why you frequently see unrealistic values like $1,025. You know and I know that nothing actually sold at that price, so where does a price like that come from? Perhaps something like this:

New York City Madison Avenue shop   $1,700
Palm Springs, CA, shop                  900
Ad in *The Antique Trader Weekly*        800
Downstate Illinois auction house         700

The average of these prices is $1,025, so that amount gets printed in a price guide. When you carry your item to a local dealer and ask $1,000 for it "because that's what the book says," you will be sadly disappointed when the highest offer you receive is $300 to $500.

There is another danger in taking price guide prices as an indicator of value. Sometimes they are too low. I've talked with experts who read price guides and say, "I'll take every one I can get at that price. It's worth five times that!" Wouldn't you hate to discover your $1,025 item could have been sold for $5,000?

General price guides list artificial numbers, *not prices you will get when you sell your things.* Like the porridge in another piece of fiction, some prices are too high, some too low, and some just right. In some cases they are deliberately skewed by an author attempting to raise or lower values within a hobby. Whether or not these prices are accurate doesn't matter if all you want is a rough idea of what something you own is worth.

Unfortunately that's not good enough for most readers. People obtain copies of my buyer directories because they want to *sell* things. Value becomes important when you go to sell something. Then, the difference between $40 and $400 becomes great. That's what makes *The World's Most Accurate Price Guide* so unusual.

This is the only general price guide which tells you *how much cash someone is going to take out of their pocket and put in yours.* Not only that, **The World's Most Accurate Price Guide tells** you *who* **exactly will put that money in your pocket.**

Best of all, if your item is not in this book and you identify yourself as a reader of *Hyman's Price Guide,* **you may contact the buyer of those items and ask.** No other price guide gives you this invitation.

Finally, a useful accurate price guide!

# Table of Contents

# Prices and Buyers

# USING THIS PRICE GUIDE

I don't particularly like price guides. I don't believe they are needed. What an item is worth is irrelevant until I'm going to sell it, and when I'm ready to sell it, I simply call an expert, tell him or her what I have and tell them to send me a check for a fair price. Then I send the item to them. It's that easy. I find out what it's "worth" when I get my check. If you don't want to sell it, then what difference does it make what some book says it's "worth"?

But forty years buying and selling antiques and collectibles has taught me that some folks feel secure when they have a book in front of them that puts a dollar value on things. Since most price guides are so inaccurate, we put this guide together so you will know what some items are *really* worth. These prices tell you how much cash you will actually put in your pocket. No other price guide does that.

You probably won't find your item in here. You probably won't find your item in *any* guide. There are billions of items, and only a small handful are listed in guides. The advantage of using *this* guide over all others is that we provide you a name and address of someone you can actually get money from...or call or write to find out more information about similar things that aren't listed.

Each page in this guide is written by one of the expert buyers you can find in *Trash or Treasure*. Each one of these people approached writing a price guide slightly differently. Some of these folks have given you long lists with prices indicated, like most price guides. The difference is, these are *real* prices because they tell you how much money they will pay..how much you will get. In some cases, buyers have given you a range of prices. The range reflects acceptable levels of condition or minor variations in the item being priced.

Since only 100 or so items can be listed on a page, a few buyers have used the opportunity to teach you about their specialty to help you determine what you have and how much it might sell for.

## SUMMARY:

**Here's how we recommend you sell your collectibles:**
1. **Find something you want to sell**
2. **Ask one of Hyman's guides to see who wants it**
    *(see this price guide or look in Trash or Treasure)*
3. **Send a letter or Sell-A-Gram** *(see pages 14-15)*
4. **Take their offer, as it will probably be accurate and fair**

# USING OTHER PRICE GUIDES

Price guides have a place.

If I didn't think so, I wouldn't have gone to such great trouble to assemble this very special price guide for you.

Three different kinds of guides are available:
    (1) general
    (2) specialty
    (3) comprehensive specialty

To use them, you need to understand what they are, how they are different, and what they can and can't do for you.

## GENERAL GUIDES

The book you are reading right now is a "general price guide." Bigger and better known general guides include those produced each year by the Kovels and *The Antique Trader*. General guides cover a variety of topics, but no one guide can cover everything. Our guide covers only a few topics. Even the giant guides with their claims of 50,000+ prices cover only a tiny handful of possible items. When you consider there have been literally billions of items manufactured that are collectible to someone, you can understand why all general guides are of limited use, particularly to amateur sellers. The truth is, most of the items you want to look up you won't find in this book or in any general guide. After 3 to 4 years, a general guide is obsolete.

General guides are created for entry level and beginning antique and flea market dealers. They buy households and large quantities of "stuff" and use these guides to get an idea of how to price. Since they handle many thousands of items, a mistake or two (or ten or one hundred) doesn't matter much in the long haul  People who buy entire estates pay so little they can afford to sell items at only a rough approximation of value. You can't afford to do that...unless of course you're terribly rich and can afford to throw away $100 bills.

After 40 years experience coast to coast, I know that many antique dealers are weekenders and amateurs...sellers of second hand goods. General price guides give them a small amount of guidance but they still make plenty mistakes. You can walk into almost any antique shop in America and find items priced for 10% to 30% of what expert buyers would be willing to pay. I've never known an expert experienced dealer who uses general price guides.

You might well ask, "Why, if experts pay so much more, don't more antique dealers sell to them?"  The best dealers do. Over the years, they have cultivated a following of expert buyers to whom they sell quickly and at high prices. Dealers who use my *Where To Sell Series* say they double and triple their overall income as a result.

# SPECIALTY GUIDES

Specialty guides are price guides on a single topic, like lighters, blue willow china, *Colt* pistols, matchcovers, etc. As with everything else in life, quality varies widely. Some outstanding specialty guides exist, while others can actually cause you to lose money.

## To evaluate a specialty price guide look for:

(1) **Pictures**: you want pictures of all major variations of pattern and shape, as well as pictures which can help you locate and identify key elements of a particular type of item.

(2) **Lots of explanatory text:** you want examples of marks, definitions of parts of an item, history of the makers and processes involved, etc. If every collectible item in a hobby can't be priced and pictured, this text can be very useful to determine rarity, estimate value, and learn how to describe your item.

(3) **Dating information:** almost all collectibles have key identifying elements which make it possible for you to date them. Information about marks, color, form and other elements all help and should be provided.

(4) **Information about grading and condition:** condition is an integral part of valuing any collectible. The standards applied by collectors and dealers within the hobby should be explained.

(5) **Authors with solid backgrounds:** look for books by folks with no less than ten years experience. I prefer those by club officers, newsletter editors, and other people in touch with many other people in their hobby. Antiques book publishers, including some of the well-known ones, have staff "writers" whose job it is to crank out books because an item is "hot" with little regard for information. If a book doesn't contain a biography of the author, beware.

(6) **An index:** books without indexes are always of less use; when a book is small, like this guide, a table of contents may suffice.

(7) **Information on how prices are determined:** you want to know the reasons an author says, "it is worth $xxx."

If the price guide you are considering has all or most of those characteristics, it is a good investment if you want to be a collector, dealer, or picker of those items. There is no substitute for information. If you'd like to see a really bad book along side a really good one, compare *Collecting Cigarette Lighters* by Wood with the very useful *Ronson: The World's Greatest Lighter* by Cummings.

Many hundreds of specialty guides are available if you live near a large bookstore willing to stock them, or if you have access to one of the three or four mail order antique book companies.

# COMPREHENSIVE SPECIALTY GUIDES

Comprehensive specialty guides are price guides on a single topic. In addition to all the characteristics described above, comprehensive guides make a serious effort to picture, describe, and/or price all or nearly all known items in a give collectible field.

Stamps and coins are two fields with well-known comprehensive specialty guides available. Comic books, Beatles memorabilia, *Avon, PEZ* dispensers, *Hot Wheels, Hummel, Gillette, Fostoria*, baseball cards, cigarette cards, presidential pin-back buttons, *Little Golden Books*, and Disneyana are among lesser known fields with outstanding comprehensive specialty guides.

People who are not expert do not tackle the enormous chore of compiling comprehensive specialty guides. Once completed, they typically become the "bibles" of their hobby. If you are planning to become a dealer, picker, or collector in any field, buy a comprehensive guide if one exists. These are indispensible works for anyone who plans to take a given topic seriously.

Specialty guides are the best to use, but they aren't possible for all topics. There can be no comprehensive guide to books because there have been millions upon millions of books, many of which don't even have established collector values. Cigar boxes (one and a half million different), folk art (where every piece is different), matchcovers (countless unrecorded numbers), and trade (advertising) cards are other examples of topics which can never have *comprehensive* guides, but which do have excellent specialty guides available now.

Some minor problems exist for users of specialty guides. They are aimed at a select audience of people seriously interested in a topic. As a result, they sometimes use a specialized vocabulary and assume certain knowledge on the part of their readers. Availability can be a problem. Many guides sell less than 3,000 copies nationwide, and some excellent books have total printings less than 1,000. Specialty guides can be difficult to find in public libraries. Libraries are short of funds and don't buy them because of their limited appeal.

# CAUTIONS ABOUT ALL GUIDES

Price guides have limitations, the greatest one being the reader. Readers have a tendency to glance at the "price" given, close the book and think they have learned something. Even worse, they will sometimes try to act on that "knowledge." If you buy a guide, any guide, **read the introductory material.**

Keep in mind that the more rare an item, the less likely it is to be listed in a price guide. If a rare item *is* listed, it is more likely to be priced inaccurately because there are fewer examples for comparison.

A sure way to lose money is to assume the price of an item similar to yours is the price of yours. Tiny variations can be big fortunes. A single letter on a coin can mean a difference of $50,000 in your pocket. Be very careful if what you have doesn't match exactly!

# "WHAT'S MY ITEM WORTH?"

No book can tell you what your item is worth, although the one you're reading right now comes as close as practical. No book can tell you because, even though collectible...even antique...you are still trying to sell second hand goods. No two second hand items are identical. The amount of money realized when something is sold depends on how, where, why, by whom and to whom it is sold.

I'd like you to get as much money as possible with a minimum of time and effort. That's what *Trash or Treasure* and this price guide are about.

The world is full of books and people who say, "Your [whatever] is worth [whatever]." But in the world of antiques and collectibles nothing has dollar value until you sell it. Only when a buyer and seller agree to a price and money changes hands is value determined. Each time something sells, its value could be more, less, or the same as the day before. In the world of second hand goods, selling is always a bit of an adventure.

For most people, setting the price is the most difficult part of selling. Selling the way I do offers you an alternative to the hassle and guesswork of pricing.

I know very little about electric trains. If I have an electric train to sell, how can I put a price on it? I can't. Not with any accuracy. I'd be as likely to underprice it as overprice it...either give it away or not be able to sell it at all.

If I don't know enough to set a selling price, who does? An expert in electric trains, that's who. For forty years I've been dealing with experts and letting them tell me what prices they will pay me. I usually accept what they offer, but sometimes don't. I usually find I make the most money by trusting an expert to make me a fair offer. The process is usually simple, quick, and profitable.

When dealing with experts I don't even need to know exactly what I have. Their years of experience enables them to tell me in seconds what could take me weeks or months of research to learn.

It is popular these days to be cynical about honesty and to assume everyone is crooked. Fortunately, that's simply not the case. The world is full of honest, knowledgeable, helpful people, a few of whom you will meet in the pages of this book. If you deal with good people, you don't need to know an item's value to get a fair price. You don't even need to know what your item is. The Midwestern lady who got $4,800 for a crock didn't have the foggiest notion of what her item was worth, except that a local antique dealer offered "$50 or $60" for it. The honest expert she dealt with (Dick Hume, page 18) evaluated her crock with an expert's eye and paid her $4,800.

Whenever you offer something for sale, a buyer will evaluate your item in terms of scarcity, desirability and condition. Dealing with an expert buyer makes it more likely you will get an accurate assessment of what you have and a reasonable estimate of fair market value.

When a buyer makes you an offer, weigh the amount of money you will get against how much you enjoy owning the object. Also consider the satisfaction of helping a collector or researcher and the comfort of knowing your cherished item will have a caring new home. More often than not, **I accept the offer, sell and move on with my life.**

**What's to keep a buyer from ripping you off?** That depends on the buyer. If you are careless about who you pick, you might be cheated. You must pick carefully.

My *Where To Sell Series* and companion price guides introduce you to the people I personally sell to. In the next few pages you'll meet some of the country's top experts in their fields: men and women who write price guides, edit newsletters and are officers in collectors' clubs. Many of these people have been at their hobbies for 20 years or more. These folks have careers and reputations at stake when they do business. If they cheat you, word will get around fast. Dishonest people do not stay in business long in the world of collectibles.

Some folks claim there is a conflict of interest in having the same person evaluate and set the price. That situation can occur, but my experience is that **I get fair prices when dealing with honest people.** And I'm confident that I'm a great many dollars ahead of selling at a yard sale, flea market, or local auction.

Fast, easy, and fair. Works for me...and tens of thousands of other people. It will work for you.

## HOW MUCH WILL A COLLECTOR OR DEALER PAY?

The following are generalizations. They are not meant to portray any particular dealer or group of dealers. They are based on years of experience, observation, reading, and reports from dealers themselves.

**A flea market dealer** usually sells lower priced goods (under $40) or sells medium priced goods (under $500) at low prices. They are seldom in a position to pay more than a few cents on a dollar. Many mall dealers (where dozens of people share stalls in warehouse-like shops) pay only slightly more.

**Shop dealers** come in all sizes, shapes specialties and skill levels, so generalizations are difficult. From a business standpoint, the general or semi-specialist shop must try to pay from 5% to 30% to survive in the face of high expenses. Shop owners make frequent mistakes because their experience is usually limited to a few fields. When they buy outside their specialty, they must pay low.

**Auction houses** exist at all levels of skill and clientele. The price you get will depend upon the quality of your item, its history, what is being auctioned the same day, when and where the auction is held, and, most important of all, who will be attracted to bid in the auction. Most sales at auctions are to dealers who will double or triple the auction price (except on very expensive items) when they sell to their customers. Prices realized at auction range from 1% to a typical 15% to 60% of what items will bring in private sale to specialists. Top flight goods will sometimes sell for 50% to 100% of value, or more.

Record prices are set at auction. Record prices are also set in private sale; those prices are not reported publically but they happen as often. Don't forget you will pay a commission to an auction house of 15% to 25% of the bid. Selling goods through an auction house does not guarantee your item will be properly identified or evaluated. Errors in evaluation and identification are a lot more frequent than the big auction houses would like you to believe. At least two good size auction houses have recently succumbed to criminal charges, legal troubles, or financial woes, so investigate any auctioneer thoroughly before turning over your goods.

**A specialty dealer** usually pays from 20% to 75% of an item's full retail value. It depends on how much money he has, how anxious he is to add your item to his inventory and how quickly he thinks your item will resell. The more expensive the item, the higher percentage of retail value you should expect. Specialty dealers will buy a wider range of items than will collectors. Too, it is very difficult to find specialty collectors, many of whom prefer to remain anonymous, buying their goods through specialty dealers.

**Collectors tend to pay the most**, between 60% and 100% (or more) of what anyone else will pay. One collector explained:

> "If I'm offered a common item, worth only $5 or $6, I'm rarely interested in paying more than a dollar or two for it, if I buy it at all. I don't want to tie up money or space with minor items. When someone offers me a $100 item, I'm willing to pay full value or even more. If it's a *very* rare item, I'm willing to set record prices to make certain I get it."

## AS STRANGE AS IT MIGHT SEEM...

When dealing with specialty dealers and collectors, **high value items are much easier for you to sell than low value items.** Items have low value because everyone who wants them has them, so demand is low. It is almost impossible, for example, to sell a $20 tin can today, but you can sell a $1,000 tin can is less than five minutes. A $2 cigar box will find no takers, whereas a $200 box will sell quickly if you know the right buyer.

## SUMMARY REPEATED:

**Here's what you do to sell your collectibles:**
   1. **Find something you want to sell**
   2. **Ask one of Hyman's guides to see who wants it**
      *(see this price guide or look in Trash or Treasure)*
   3. **Send a letter or Sell-A-Gram** *(see pages 14-15)*
   4. **Take their offer, as it will probably be accurate and fair**

# CONTACTING BUYERS

## WHO ARE THE PEOPLE WHO WROTE THIS GUIDE?

The people who wrote the prices in this book average more than 15 years experience and are well known in their fields. Many of them are full time antique dealers and auctioneers. Six are doctors, dentists or psychiatrists who have made a lifetime study of their hobby. Because they are experienced they can tell you in seconds what you have and how much cash it is likely to raise for you. The most important characteristic of the people you'll meet in this guide is that **they all have made the commitment to treat you fairly.** That's why these are the people I personally do business with.

## PHONES AND FAXES

**Phones are a great convenience** when you want to sell in a hurry, have large quantities or have complicated things to describe.

> Always have the item in front of you when you call.
> Be conscious of time differences. If you live on the East coast, don't call California before noon.
> Don't call collect.
> If you leave a message on an answering machine, speak slowly and clearly. Include your name, phone number, best time to call, and information about why you are calling.

**One of the many advantages of fax** is that you can do it any time of the day or night. Since a fax is a printed piece of paper, the person on the other end can deal with it at his or her convenience, perhaps after looking up information for you etc. Fax also gives you a printed record of correspondence and agreements.

## PHOTOCOPIES AND PHOTOGRAPHS

**Photocopies are made with a Xerox© type machine.** I suggest you make a photocopy of what you have to sell because it is the cheapest and easiest way to describe most items. Objects such as knives, small dolls, badges, medals, pipes, even pistols, will usually photocopy well enough for a buyer to know what you have. Copies are especially useful for describing china patterns and paper goods. Color copies are an unnecessary expense in most cases.

**Photographs are taken with a camera.** The best photos are close-ups taken with a 35mm camera. If you do not have a camera, perhaps a friend who does can take pictures for you. Polaroid and snapshot cameras frequently do not provide enough detail to be useful to a potential buyer.

## SELL-A-GRAMS

**Use the form found on the next two pages.** You may either make Xerox© copies of it (preferably on yellow paper) or use it as a guide for providing information in a letter. Let people know you found them in this guidebook. Always include a Stamped Self-Addressed Envelope if you want a reply.

SENDER

- [ ] The item is for sale for $_____ plus shipping.
- [ ] The item is for sale. I am an amateur seller and would like you to make an offer.
- [ ] The item may be for sale if the price is sufficient. Would you like to make an offer?
- [ ] The item is not for sale, but I am willing to pay a fee to learn its value.

To assist you to evaluate the item, I am enclosing a:
[ ] Sample [ ] Photocopy [ ] Photo [ ] Tracing [ ] Sketch [ ] Rubbing [ ] Nothing

This is to certify that, to the best of my knowledge, the item is genuine and as described.
Buyer has a 5 day examination period during which the item may be returned for any reason.

Signature: _____ Date: _____

[ ] Answer Requested (SASE enclosed).          [ ] No answer needed.

BUYER'S RESPONSE:

# SELL-A-GRAM

from a reader of Tony Hyman's

**TO:**

**FROM:**

**Phone:** ( )

**I have the following item:**

Remember to include the (1) shape, (2) colors, (3) dimensions, and (4) all names, dates, and marks. Re-read pages 10-14 and and any text or entry notes for selling what you have.

**It's condition is:**

List all chips, repairs, cracks, dents, fading, scratches, rips, tears, creases, holes, stains, and foxing. Note any missing pages, parts, or paint.

# Mesh Purses

We are fascinated by **painted mesh purses** made in the 1920's and 1930's. Mesh purses were made with very small individual metal links and painted with colorful stenciled designs. The value of these purses lies in the aesthetic appeal of the design on the mesh and whether or not they possess certain unusual features. Some painted designs are attractive, but rather plain or common. Higher prices are offered for bags with striking designs. Other bags have a plain design, but some uncommon feature that sets them apart. Purses with a combination of imaginative painted designs and remarkable features are even more desirable. Some of the unusual features and striking designs we look for include:

- Scenes, animals, or people
- Elaborate Art Deco designs
- Cartoon characters like Mickey Mouse, Betty Boop or Winnie-the-Pooh
- Ornate frames with 'jewels' or stones
- Exceptionally large (6"x10") or small (2"x3")
- Frames made of bakelite
- An attached or built-in compact ("vanity bags")

*Left to right*

*Corner compact,     $350+*

*Mandalian floral $175-225*

*Ornate frame     $125-175*

*Dragon            $300-350*

We will consider exceptional purses with minor wear or a few disconnected links, but others must be in top condition to receive consideration. We are looking for the most desirable pieces in the best condition to add to our personal collection where they will be admired and cherished for years to come.

| | |
|---|---|
| Whiting & Davis corner compact vanity bag | $350+ |
| Whiting & Davis swinging compact vanity bag | 350+ |
| Whiting & Davis double bag mesh vanity | 350+ |
| R & G vanity bag, cloisonne lid & octagonal top | 300-350 |
| Purse with Betty Boop painted on mesh | 350+ |
| Child's purse, Mickey Mouse painted on mesh | 350+ |
| Child's purse, Winnie-the-Pooh & Tigger on mesh | 175-225 |
| Child's purse (2"x3" to 3"x4"), plain design on mesh | 50-75 |
| Child's purse (2"x3" to 3"x4"), figural design on mesh | 75-125 |
| Child's purse; mesh bottom, round frame & silk top | 100-125 |
| Miniature rosary bag with enameled metal lid | 125-150 |
| Purse with outstanding Art Deco design on mesh (5"x7") | 100-150 |
| Purse with unusual or ornate frame (5"x8") | 125-175 |
| Mandalian purse, swans or deer painted on mesh | 150-200 |
| Whiting & Davis purse, snow-covered log cabin scene | 150-200 |
| Mandalian purse, floral design & painted frame (5"xl0") | 175-225 |
| Whiting & Davis purse, dragon painted on mesh (5"x7") | 300-350 |
| Purse with 5 colored glass stones set in mesh (both sides) | 250-300 |
| Mandalian purse, bracelet style self-opening top | 125-175 |
| Purse with bakelite frame | 225-250 |

# Ladies' Figural Compacts

**Figural compacts** are compacts in which the case is in the shape of an object such as a roulette wheel, a globe or a silver dollar. We do not purchase conventional round or square compacts even if they have an embossed, engraved or applied figure on the lid.

Scratches, dents or excessively worn finishes will cause us to eliminate even the most sought after compacts from consideration. We prefer that the contents and mirror be intact, but will consider hard-to-find pieces that are not complete. Highest prices are paid for compacts in unused condition with original powder, rouge, puffs and box.

| | |
|---|---|
| Bird by Elgin (silver & gold color) | $700+ |
| Guitar by Samaral | 150-200 |
| Beach Umbrella | 125-175 |
| Roulette wheel by Majestic | 75-90 |
| Globe by Kigu (silver & gold color) | 150-200 |
| Globe by Kigu (musical) | 275-350 |
| Silver dollar | 75-100 |
| Jockey's cap | 100-150 |
| Christmas ornament ball (w/stripe) | 75-100 |
| Padlock | 60-80 |
| Padlock, enameled | 100-120 |
| Fox or Cat face (marked Italy) | 100-150 |
| Book by Raquel (red or green) | 50-75 |
| Binoculars by Wadsworth | 100-150 |
| Drum by Charbert | 125-150 |
| Hand w/painted nails by Volupte | 125-150 |
| Navy officer's cap (blue & white) | 40-50 |
| Liberty Bell | 100-125 |
| Teddy Bear by Schuco (red) | 450-600 |
| Tambourine (bullfight scene on top) | 150-200 |
| Golf ball | 25-35 |

*Bird $700+*
*Guitar $150-200*
*Beach Umbrella $125-175*
*Drum $125-150*

# Celluloid-Covered Boxes & Albums

We collect **Victorian era boxes** which held collars and cuffs, brush, comb, and mirror sets, gloves, shaving sets, neckties, etc. **Photograph and autograph albums** are also wanted. The boxes and albums we collect have a picture on the front or top that is covered with a thin layer of clear celluloid. Usually, colorful print paper and/or velvet material covers the rest of the piece. The highest prices are paid for those that have close-up views of ladies or children. Those with French or Colonial attired people are much less valuable. We do not purchase "French Ivory" celluloid boxes, solid celluloid dresser sets, or pieces without a picture on top. Nothing will be considered that isn't in top condition, that has cracked celluloid, stains, or missing hardware. Interior condition is not as critical. Color photo usually needed.

### Boxes & Albums w/ladies or children

| | |
|---|---|
| Box, large | $85-200 |
| Box, medium | 50-100 |
| Box, small | 40-75 |
| Autograph album | 25-75 |
| Photograph album | 75-175 |
| Photograph album, musical | 125-250 |

*Autograph album $25-75*

| **Prices Paid by:** | Mike & Sherry Miller | |
|---|---|---|
| | 303 Holliday Ave. | (217) 253-4991 |
| | Tuscola, IL 61953 | email: miller@tuscola.net |

# Stoneware & Crocks

*Birds of all types – $200 to $3,500*

There has been stoneware, redware and related items made since the early 1700's. These things were made to be used on an everyday basis. They were used for the daily table for eating, drinking, making butter, or for holding whiskey, wine or apple cider. You name it, it had a good use. These items are collectors items today for their form, their decorations, and their overall appeal. These were made all over the country, especially here in N.J. and N.Y., where they found great clay for the making these items. The value is in the decoration. The greater the blue, the more you will be paid. Condition means a lot. Cracks, chips, etc., hurt the value. Pieces with flowers or birds are the most common. We pay a premium for stoneware with animals, ships, peacocks, houses and other odd decorations. Remember, the greater the blue the more money we pay. Look for pieces that are stamped with the maker's mark. We also want Southern pottery, decorated redware, etc. We will pay top dollar for any jug, crock, pitcher, churn or canning jar with unusual decorations.

For pieces with these decorations, we will pay the following
(These are all blue decorated done in a blue cobalt):

| | |
|---|---|
| Deer | $1,500-6,000+ |
| People | 2,500-10,000+ |
| Trees & houses | 1,000-3,000+ |
| Peacocks | 2,500-5,000+ |
| Birds | 200-5,000+ |
| Florals | 100-1,000+ |
| Man in the moon | 1,000-2,500+ |
| Lions | 3,000-10,000+ |
| Horses | 2,000-5,000+ |
| Trains | 10,000+ |
| Ships | 1,500-4,000+ |
| Flags | 1,000-10,000+ |
| Decorated inkwells | 500-2,500+ |
| Flasks | 300-3,500+ |

*People – $2,500 to $10,000+*

Look for names like BENNINGTON VT, COWDEN & WILCOX PA, T. HARRINGTON LYONS NY, FULPER BROTHERS FLEMMINGTON, NJ, FT. EDWARD POTTERY CO. NY or any pottery stamped with the name of any Southern or Mid-Western pottery.

Also look for any pieces marked as having been made in N.J. or N.Y., especially Rockingham pitchers, for which I'll pay from $250-5,000+.

Decorated redware plates, bowls and pitchers colored in a yellow, green slip are wanted. They range from simple yellow decorations to names on them and the best ones are multi-colored.

Paying top dollar for all pottery, redware, or stoneware plates with scenes, animals, etc. Any plate or bowl with horses, people, dates is worth $1,000-$15,000+.

The better ones are usually from Pennsylvania or Southern U.S. Some made by the Pennsylvania Dutch have German writing. Condition is very important.

Deer - $1,500 to $6,000

Plates $1,000 to $15,000

**Prices Paid by:** R.C. Hume
P.O. Box 281
Bay Head, NJ 08742     (732) 899-8707
Send good photos and describe the condition for accurate estimates of value.

# Glass Paperweights

Top quality glass paperweights and related items have been made in three distinct periods since the early 1840's. A good paperweight is made of clear glass, with a colored design suspended inside. The basic types are:

**Millefiori:** has thin "Christmas candy" like slices of colored glass, which may be arranged in a variety of different designs, or simply packed closely together.

**Lampwork:** realistic or stylized representations of flowers, reptiles, insects or fruit, etc., which are surrounded by clear glass.

*Lampwork bouquet by Chris Bussini, mid 1980's $400 to $800*

**Sulphides:** (cameo incrustations) a white "ceramic", or colored silver or gold foil depiction of a famous person, historical or Biblical event, or military insignia.

The shape of a good weight is usually a slightly flattened sphere with a flat (actually slightly concave) base. The surface may be cut with "windows". Rarer weights sometimes are covered with one or two layers of colored glass, cut with "windows", through which the design is visible.

**VALUE:** The value of a glass paperweight is determined by a number of factors, the most important being; artist or factory, rarity, design, beauty, craftsmanship and condition.

## CLASSIC PERIOD 1845-1870

Made in France, England, the United States, Bohemia and Venice. Rare exceptional weights can be worth as much as $50,000., with an average weight bringing around $1,000. Most antique weights are not signed or dated. Those that are will contain a tiny initial B, C, J, IGW, SL, etc. inside the design, with or without a date. Legitimate dates are, 1845, 1846, 1847, 1848, 1849, 1852 (and inverted appearing as 1825), 1853, and 1858. Other nineteenth century dates are fake, most often appearing in Italian weights made during the past few decades.

## INTERMEDIATE YEARS 1870-1950

Very few good paperweights were made during this period. Those that were, feature three dimensional, realistic lampwork, flowers, fruit, butterflies and reptiles. In the late nineteenth century good weights were made by Mt. Washington Glass Company in the United States, Pantin in France, and an unknown maker most likely in Russia. Another type of weight featuring crimp flowers was made by several individuals in the Millville, NJ area in the early 1900's. The Pantin and Mt. Washington weights are often large, 4" or more in diameter. "Millville" weights have a clear glass foot or pedestal. The "Russian" weights are often flat, rectangular plaques containing flowers or fruit. We will pay up to $2,000 for the best Millville weights, and from $5,000 to $20,000 for good examples from the other makers. Weights from this period are not signed or dated.

## CONTEMPORARY 1953 TO DATE

Most top quality contemporary weights are signed internally or on the surface with the artists' initials or name.   Listed below are the names of the makers we are most interested in purchasing.  Prices paid range from $50 to over $5,000 depending on the maker and design.

| | | |
|---|---|---|
| Ayotte, Rick | Kontes, James | Stankard, Paul |
| Baccarat | Knotes, Nontas | Tarsitano, Debbie |
| Banford, Bob | Labino, Dominick | Tarsitano, Delmo |
| Banford, Bobby | Littleton, Harvey | Trabucco, David & Jon |
| Banford, Ray | Manson, William | Trabucco, Victor |
| Buzzini, Chris | Parsley, Johne | Whitefriars |
| Donofrio, Jim | Perthshire | Whittemore, Francis |
| Grubb, Randall | Rosenfeld, Ken | Ysart, Paul |
| "J" Glass | Saint Louis | |
| Kaziun, Charles | Smith, Gordon | |

### Paperweight related items wanted

Other glass objects incorporating paperweight decorating techniques in the base or body of the object are also wanted.  These objects include: bottles, boxes, candlesticks, cups, doorknobs, goblets, lamps, letter presses, mantel ornaments, marbles, obelisks, perfumes, plates, plaques, snuff mulls and tumblers.

Paperweight literature, auction catalogues and books also wanted.

Magazines with articles about paperweights are worth $1 each.  Auction catalogues devoted to glass paperweights are worth from $1-5 each.  Books about paperweights are worth from $5-100.

### NOT WANTED:

**Chinese weights**
(glass often is greasy feeling and appears yellowish, design contains "school bus" yellow)

**Advertising weights**

**Murano weights**
(usually have perfectly flat base)

**Souvenir weights**

**Weights with fake dates** (before 1845, or in the 1860's, 70's or 80's

**Weights with large bubbles & swirls of color in the design**

**Cute shapes** (dogs, cats, etc.)

**Colored apples and pears on a clear "cookie" base** are sometimes of interest. If you have one of these, take a good picture and inquire.

---

### Books about paperweights available

| | |
|---|---|
| Old Glass paperweights of Southern New Jersey | $20 |
| Paperweights of the 19th and 20th Centuries | 60 |
| The Jokelson Collection of Antique Cameo Incrustation | 60 |

Available postage paid by sending a check to:
Papier Presse, PO Box 6269, Statesville, NC  28687-6269

---

**Prices Paid by:**  Paul Dunlop
PO Box 6269
Statesville, NC  28687
(800) 227-1996      Within NC :  (704) 871-2626

# Cast Iron Cookware

Griswold is the most popular cast iron cookware collectible. However, there is interest in unusual pieces by makers such as Wagner, Piqua, Favorite, Wapak, G.F. Filley and Martin. I am also interested in unmarked coffee roasters, broilers and baking pans. Griswold skillets must be marked with the large logo (about 3″ dia.) or ERIE. Prices quoted are for black iron. Nickle finish are worth about 25% less.

Pieces must be in good condition, free from cracks, chips, and crusted rust. Light rust and burned grease is OK. Please do not clean them. I prefer to clean them myself!

Griswold skillets number 3, 6 & 8 are worth $5 unless marked Al Carder, Cliff Cornell, or Victor, in which case they are worth $30-150. A #5 Victor is worth $250.

## GRISWOLD

### Muffin/Gem/Cornstick Pans

| | | |
|---|---|---|
| #2800 | Wheat or corn | $1,000 |
| #2700 | Wheat or corn | 250 |
| #28 | ERIE single loaf | 1,000 |
| #26 | ERIE double loaf | 500 |
| #1 | Single Vienna roll | 500 |
| #2 | Double Vienna roll | 300 |
| #4 | (957) Vienna roll | 200 |
| #280 | Wheat or corn | 500 |
| #270 | Wheat or corn | 150 |
| #50 | Hearts star | 500 |
| #100 | Hearts star | 250 |
| #19 | Golf ball | 250 |
| #9 | Golf ball | 85 |
| #240 | Turks head | 150 |
| #130 | Turks head | 230 |
| #140 | Turks head | 100 |
| #13 | Turks head | 500 |
| #14 | Turks head | 350 |
| #1 | | 100 |
| #3 | | 250 |
| #5 | | 250 |

*Erie No. 28  $1000*

### Toys - "0" or "00" Size
(may be marked "2" or "4")

| | |
|---|---|
| Griddle | $200 |
| Dutch Oven | 200 |
| Tea kettle | 250 |
| Waffle iron | 1,000 |
| Pup #30 | 150 |
| Aluminum toys | 50 |

### Skillets (Large Logo)

| | |
|---|---|
| #0 | 40 |
| #1 | 1,000 |
| #2 | 200 |
| #4 | 35 |
| #5 | 10 |
| #7 | 8 |
| #9 | 12 |
| #10 | 25 |
| #11 | 75 |
| #12 | 45 |
| #13 | 500 |
| #14 | 75 |
| #14 w/bail handle | 500 |
| #20 | 400 |
| All In One (3 sec) | 250 |
| Spider logo "ERIE" | 700 |
| Oval skillet #15 | 200 |
| Oval skillet #13 | 200 |
| Double skillet (top & btm) | 50 |

### Skillet Covers

| | |
|---|---|
| #3 - #9 | $25 |
| #10 & 12 | 50 |
| #11 & 14 | 150 |
| #13 & 20 | 500 |

### Round Griddles
(20 more for Diamond logo)

| | |
|---|---|
| #6 | $50 |
| #10 | 25 |
| #14 | 35 |
| #16 | 45 |
| Vapor griddle | 150 |

### Dutch Ovens

| | |
|---|---|
| #6 | $100 |
| #7 | 40 |
| #10 | 50 |
| #11 | 100 |
| #12 | 250 |
| #13 | 250 |

### Oval Roasters
(add $25 with trivet)

| | |
|---|---|
| #3 | $350 |
| #5 | 200 |
| #7 | 200 |
| #9 | 350 |

### Waffle Irons

| | |
|---|---|
| #6 | $150 |
| #7 | 45 |
| Hearts star #18 | 100 |
| Hearts star #19 | 200 |
| Square #s "0", "00", #1, #2 | 250 |

### Cake Molds

| | |
|---|---|
| Santa | $450 |
| Rabbit | 175 |
| Lamb | 65 |
| Bundt | 500 |

*Wagner Wire No. 1  $500*

### Miscellaneous

| | |
|---|---|
| 5 in 1 breakfast skillet | $100 |
| 110 skillet griddle | 50 |
| Double broiler | 150 |
| Coffee grinder | 400 |
| Alum bread slicer | 200 |
| Dutch Oven rack (5 tier) | 750 |
| Dutch Oven rack (3 tier) | 500 |
| Griddle rack | 200 |
| Skillet rack | 125 |
| Sun dial | 200 |
| Loaf pan | 200 |
| Loaf pan w/cover | 350 |
| Coffee roaster | 400 |
| Wafer iron w/base | 225 |

### WAGNER Ware Gem Pans

| | |
|---|---|
| #1 Handled Gem pan | $500 |
| Style "M" 4 section | 350 |
| STyle "N" 4 section | 350 |

### Wapak

| | |
|---|---|
| Indian Head skillet | $40-250 |

*I am not interested in:
   #8 Dutch Ovens or numbers 10, 11, 22 or 273 muffin or bread stick pans.
*Also Wanted – Trade Catalogs which includes cast iron cookware     $200+

---

**Prices Paid by:**   David G. "Pan Man" Smith
                      PO Box B
                      Perrysburg, NY 14129
                         (716) 532-5154        DGSpanman@aol.com

---

# Silverware & Holloware

Silverware means knives, forks, spoons, etc.   Holloware is trays, teapots, plates, bowls, etc.

## SILVERWARE & HOLLOWARE - 5 BASIC TYPES

(1.) Sterling  (2.) Silverplate  (3.) Stainless  (4.) Pewter  (5.) Dirilyte (gold color)

**Sterling** is marked "sterling" or *"925/1000"*.

**Silverplate** has the look of sterling but not the marks of sterling. Common marks are *[(any word) and "plate"]*, *"Wm Rogers,"* *"1847 Rogers Bros,"* *"EPNS"* and *"Holmes & Edwards."* Silverplate has silver only on the surface, so use may cause the silver to be worn through to the base metal, hence worth considerably less.

**Stainless** is marked *"stainless," "18/8"* or only with the manufacturer's name.

**Pewter** is marked *"pewter"* if it is marked at all.

**Dirilyte** (gold color) is marked *"Dirilyte"*.

**Value is determined by** a combination of the following: pattern, maker, condition, and the size/style/version of piece. Dented knife handles, pitted knife blades, monograms, and excessive wear all detract from value.

**Valuation Guideline For Silverware** (MOST fall into this range)

        Sterling is worth $5 to $50 per piece.

        Stainless, Silverplate, Pewter, or Dirilyte are worth $0.05 to $1 per piece.

**Valuation Guideline For Holloware** (MOST fall into this range)

        Sterling is worth $5 to $50,000 per piece.

        Silverplate, Stainless, Pewter or Dirilyte are worth $1 to $100 per piece.

Restaurant grade & promotional silverware & holloware have no resale value.

MidweSterling buys and sells all silverware and holloware.  MidweSterling offers a repair service including knife reblading and disposal damage repair.

| Prices Paid by: | MidweSterling | (816) 454-1990 |
|---|---|---|
| | 4311 NE Vivion, Dept. HY | Fax  (816) 454-1605 |
| | Kansas City, MO  64119-2890 | Closed Wednesday & Sunday |

# Eggbeaters, Mixers, Cream Whips, Churns

I am a serious and advanced collector of rare and unusual kitchen mixing devices. I am always searching for and buying prized examples of mixing ingenuity to add to my personal collection. I will buy one or a collection if they are complete and in very good or better condition and working order. Top conditions means top $dollar$.

I am primarily searching for eggbeaters/mixers dating from 1859 to 1910. Many, if not most, will be cast-iron and can be hand-held (in a variety of styles - rotary or crank, archimedean plunger, squeeze, etc) others clamp-on, mount-on the wall, and some have glass or tin containers. There are some that you pull on a rope, chain or ratchet, and some are water powered. I don't buy electric or common beaters from the 1920's to date as a rule. Nothing with plastic or stainless steel is wanted.

Listed below are some of the beaters I am always searching for and the prices I will pay if they meet the above criteria. Most are marked with a name and or date. Some rare ones have no markings so a photo or very complete description may be necessary. If in doubt, just write or call. It may be profitable for you to also read the "miscellaneous" category below for "go-withs" I also purchase.

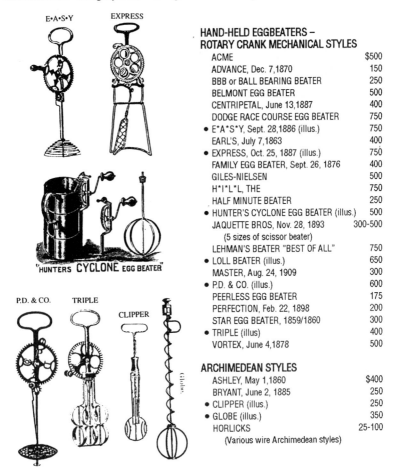

E•A•S•Y    EXPRESS

"HUNTERS CYCLONE EGG BEATER"

P.D. & CO.    TRIPLE    CLIPPER

### HAND-HELD EGGBEATERS – ROTARY CRANK MECHANICAL STYLES

| | |
|---|---|
| ACME | $500 |
| ADVANCE, Dec. 7,1870 | 150 |
| BBB or BALL BEARING BEATER | 250 |
| BELMONT EGG BEATER | 500 |
| CENTRIPETAL, June 13,1887 | 400 |
| DODGE RACE COURSE EGG BEATER | 750 |
| • E*A*S*Y, Sept. 28,1886 (illus.) | 750 |
| EARL'S, July 7,1863 | 400 |
| • EXPRESS, Oct. 25, 1887 (illus.) | 750 |
| FAMILY EGG BEATER, Sept. 26, 1876 | 400 |
| GILES-NIELSEN | 500 |
| H*I*L*L, THE | 750 |
| HALF MINUTE BEATER | 250 |
| • HUNTER'S CYCLONE EGG BEATER (illus.) | 500 |
| JAQUETTE BROS, Nov. 28, 1893 | 300-500 |
| (5 sizes of scissor beater) | |
| LEHMAN'S BEATER "BEST OF ALL" | 750 |
| • LOLL BEATER (illus.) | 650 |
| MASTER, Aug. 24, 1909 | 300 |
| • P.D. & CO. (illus.) | 600 |
| PEERLESS EGG BEATER | 175 |
| PERFECTION, Feb. 22, 1898 | 200 |
| STAR EGG BEATER, 1859/1860 | 300 |
| • TRIPLE (illus) | 400 |
| VORTEX, June 4,1878 | 500 |

### ARCHIMEDEAN STYLES

| | |
|---|---|
| ASHLEY, May 1,1860 | $400 |
| BRYANT, June 2, 1885 | 250 |
| • CLIPPER (illus.) | 250 |
| • GLOBE (illus.) | 350 |
| HORLICKS | 25-100 |
| (Various wire Archimedean styles) | |

## WALL-MOUNTED or CLAMP-ON BEATERS and CHURNS

| | |
|---|---|
| KEYSTONE MFG.CO. 1885 (4 varieties) | $250-500 |
| ● MONROE,E.P. or MONROE BROS. | |
| 1859/1860 (illus.) | 800 |
| MONITOR, June 18, 1866 | 800 |
| ● SILVER & CO, #5 or #6 (illus.) | 450 |
| ● UNIVERSAL MAYONNAISE MIXER (illus.) | 350 |
| UNIVERSAL CHURNS with glass containers | |
| (4 sizes) | #15 500 |
| | #25 300 |
| | #35 300 |
| | #45 400 |

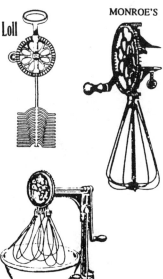

MONROE'S

Loll

## EGG BEATERS, MIXERS and CHURNS with GLASS CONTAINERS

| | |
|---|---|
| BUTTER-FLY CHURN (two sizes) | $200 |
| DAZEY BUTTER CHURN (various sizes): | |
| 1 QT. or #10 | 750-1,000 |
| 2 qt. or #20 | 150 |
| 3 qt. or #30 | 200 |
| ● E-Z MIXER (illus.) | 400 |
| GLOBE CREAM BEATER, June 11,1907 | 400 |
| HOLT-LYON SCREW-ON BEATERS (various sizes) | |
| –on original embossed glass jars | 250-500 |
| –tops only | 100-200 |
| JEWEL BEATER MIXER WHIPPER | |
| (if complete) | 500 |
| KING EGG BEATER, May 13,1884 | 800 |

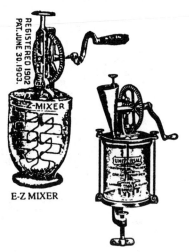

SILVER'S

## TIN SYLLABUB CHURNS "PLUNGER" ACTIONS

Only those marked with names and/or dates.

| | |
|---|---|
| BON-TON, 09-14-1875 | $75 |
| LIGHTNING EGG BEATER | |
| (made by Wm. Redheffer) | 175 |
| OVEE VACUUM BUTTER MAKER | 90 |
| PRATT'S EGG BEATER, 11-6-1866 | 175 |
| SALTMAN'S COLUMBIA, 7-10-1894 | 50 |
| STAR EGG BEATER, 10-03-1871 | 150 |
| SURPRISE | 60 |
| TILDEN'S PATENT, 8-01-1865 | 150 |

## MISCELLANEOUS GO-WITHS

| | |
|---|---|
| Mixing spoon with "propeller" in bowl | 50 |
| Tin egg separators with advertising | 10-20 |
| Tin biscuit cutter | 150 |
| –Egg Baking powder | |
| Advertising pot scrapers | 35-125 |
| (made of tin, steel or cast iron) | |
| Pre-1900 Trade cards or catalogs featuring | |
| egg beaters or apple parers | 5-100 |

E-Z MIXER

SEND CLEAR PHOTOS WITH
PHONE NUMBER AND NOTES
ABOUT MARKINGS, SIZE,
CONDITIONS AND DEFECTS FOR
QUICKEST RESPONSE.

**Prices Paid by:** Reid Cooper
32942 Josheroo Court
Temecula, CA 92592
(909) 506-3348. Please leave name and number only. I will return all calls.

# Banks • Toys • Clocks

## STILL BANKS

| | |
|---|---|
| Hippo | $1,000-2,500 |
| Rhino | 250-500 |
| Painted Buildings | 100-1,000 |

### Cast Iron or Painted Tin

| | |
|---|---|
| Small cast iron figures | $100-1,000 |
| Boston State House | 750-1,500 |
| Palace | 750-2,250 |
| Old South Church | 750-2,000 |
| Eagle with shield | 500-900 |
| Man who looks like a frog | 500-2,000 |

**No reproduction banks are wanted.**

## MECHANICAL BANKS

| | |
|---|---|
| Acrobat | $500-4,000 |
| Atlas bank | 500-2,500 |
| Bad accident | 500-2,000 |
| Baby elephant | 500-2,000 |
| Bill E. Gien | 100-300 |
| Bowling alley bank | 1,000-10,000 |
| Boy in birds nest | 500-7,000 |
| Bread winners bank | 1,000-12,000 |
| Bull dog | 500-20,000 |
| Butting buffalo | 500-2,000 |
| Calonuty | 1,000-7,000 |
| Cat and mouse | 500-2,000 |
| Chimpanzee | 500-2,500 |
| Chivomon | 500-2,000 |
| Clown banks depend on type | 500-5,000 |
| Confectionery | 500-5000 |
| Cupola | 500-4,000 |
| Baseball (Darktown battery) | 500-4,000 |
| Watermelon with man | 500-4,000 |
| Dentist | 500-2,000 |
| Ding dong bell | 250-1,500 |
| Elephants (type?) | 250-4,000 |
| Freedmans | 10,000-50,000 |
| Giant | 200-3,500 |
| Girl skipping rope | 5,000-25,000 |
| Hen & chicken | 500-1,500 |
| Home bank | 500-1,500 |
| Horse race | 500-4,500 |
| Jonah & whale | 500-3,000 |
| Little Mae | 500-3,000 |
| Magician | 500-2,500 |
| Mommy & child | 500-4,750 |
| Merry-go-round | 2,500-12,500 |
| Mason | 500-4,000 |
| Milking cow | 500-6,000 |
| Mikado | 500-12,500 |
| Monkey (type?) | 250-3,000 |
| North Pole | 250-3,000 |
| Organ grinder (type?) | 250-4,500 |
| Panorama bank | 500-7,000 |
| Paddy | 250-5,000 |
| Picture gallery | 1,250-12,500 |
| Presto bank | 100-2,000 |
| Pug dog | 100-5,000 |
| Roller skating | 1,000-10,000 |
| Santa Claus | 500-4,000 |
| Dog & tree | 500-2,500 |
| Man shooting bird | 1,000-5,000 |
| Man stealing chickens | 1,000-5,000 |
| Turtle | 500-1,500 |
| Uncle Sam | 500-5,000 |

*A Calamity Bank*
*circa 1905.*
*$7,500*

*Cottage Bank*
*(8 sided)*
*circa 1880.*
*$1,250*

*Bank*
*circa 1895.*
*$300*

*The Chinaman Bank*
*circa 1885.*
*$4,000*

No J.N. banks are wanted.
I will buy **broken banks** for parts.
Call for other undescribed banks and
   talk to me about bank condition, etc.!

## OTHER BANK ITEMS
I will buy boxes, catalogs and trade cards
   of banks still and mechanical.
**CONTAINERS** the banks were packed in:

| | |
|---|---|
| Wooden packaging boxes | $200-2,000 |
| Cardboard packaging boxes | 100-1,000 |
| PHOTOS of children with banks | 100-1,000 |

## MULTICOLORED ADVERTISING CARDS

| | |
|---|---|
| Picture gallery bank | $500-2,500 |
| Watch dog safe bank | 500-2,500 |
| Trick dog bank | 400-2,000 |
| Baseball bank | 400-1,600 |
| One color advertising flyers | 25-100 |

**No reproduction cards are wanted.**

## CATALOGS OF BANK COMPANIES

| | |
|---|---|
| J & E Stevens, Cromwell, CT | $100-500 |
| Kyser & Rex, Phila., PA | 100-500 |
| Shepard Hardware, Buffalo, NY | 100-500 |

## MOBY DICK (actual book)

| | |
|---|---|
| 1st edition, U.S. | $4,500-9,000 |
| 1st edition, British | 10,000 |
| 1930 edition, Chicago lakeside with case | 750-1,250 |

## SCRIMSHAW
Whale scrimshaw only!
Wanted 1820-1900

| | |
|---|---|
| Whale tooth scrimshaw | $250-10,000 |
| Boxes with inlay | 250-2,000 |
| Swifts | 250-8,000 |
| Kitchen implements | 250-7,500 |

Must be old and interesting. Erotic scrimshaw
desired. (Only American, no netsuke.)
No modern. Pre-1900 desired.

## CLOCKS (Only old clocks wanted)
Old 1860-1880 cast iron, painted.
Blinking Eye Clock

| | |
|---|---|
| Elf | $500-2,000 |
| Dog | 500-1,500 |
| Man on keg of beer | 500-2,000 |
| Dancing black lady | 500-2,000 |
| Man playing banjo | 500-1,500 |
| Lion | 500-1,250 |

## DOUBLE DIAL CLOCK
tells time, day, date, month, day of week

| | |
|---|---|
| Ithaca, Ingraham, Seth Thomas | $500-5,000 |
| Early American banjo clocks | 500-2,500 |

## CATALOGUES OF DOUBLE DIAL CLOCKS

| | |
|---|---|
| Early clock catalogues | $100-400 |

No repros, fakes, or electric.
   Only American pre-1910.

$750

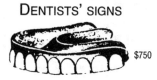

$750

## BOOK SIGNS

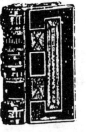

$750

*Topsey. One Day Clock circa 1870. $1,500*

*Eight-day timepiece circa 1870. $1,500*

*Office Calendar circa 1875. $2,000*

## SAFES 1870-1920

I like small safes, less than 30" high with lots of pinstripping and a small painted prcture in vignette. Value depends on conditions, pinstripping, color (white, burgundy a premium color) and picture. Must be from the 1870-1920 period. Do not desire large safes larger than 30". Especially want a small, round headed safe.

| | |
|---|---|
| Small safes | $250-1250 |
| | |
| Toy cast iron safe banks | |
| Painted | $100-300 |
| ??? | 100-300 |
| | |
| Catalogs offering toy or real safes | 50-200 |

## LEVER SEALS 1860-1920

Especially want cast iron figural ones. Must be ornate, no rust and in working order. Plain looking seals not wanted unless the seal itself is very ornate or of unusual company or group: KKK, Coca Cola, whore house, toy concern, etc. Sample prices paid:

| | |
|---|---|
| Ram's head | $50-150 |
| Eagle | 50-250 |
| Toad | 50-250 |
| Salamander | 50-250 |

## EARLY AMERICAN TIN TOYS 1860-1900

| | |
|---|---|
| Pull & Wind Up (Clockworks) | |
| Monitor (battleship) | $1,000-4,000 |
| Omnibus (larger the better) | 2,000-10,000 |
| Fire Toys | |
| Wagon, ladder | 1,000-4,000 |
| Pumper | 1,000-4,000 |
| Chariot with bank | 1,000-4,000 |
| Boats | |
| Riverboat, paddle boat | 1,000-6,000 |
| Monitor | 1,000-4,000 |
| Animals | 100-600 |
| Animals in hoops | 100-750 |
| People | |
| Black man playing banjo | 1,000-10,000 |
| Black man playing bones | 1,000-10,000 |
| Black man playing tambourine | 1,000,10,000 |
| Horsedrawn | 200-2,000 |
| Buck board | 500-1,500 |
| Clockwork fabric covered | |
| Toys | 1,000-5,000 |
| Tin building banks | |
| The more ornate the better | 100-1,000 |

Harris Bank circa 1900. $475

*Mechanical Hand Velocepede circa 1888. $2500*

*Small Steamboat circa 1880. $1,250*

*Hose Carriage circa 1880. $2,750*

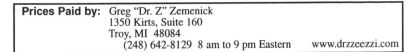

**Prices Paid by:** Greg "Dr. Z" Zemenick
1350 Kirts, Suite 160
Troy, MI  48084
(248) 642-8129  8 am to 9 pm Eastern     www.drzzeezzi.com

# Toy Guns - Cap & BB

**Substantial rewards paid** for most older air rifles with iron cocking levers (use a magnet). Also will pay well for all related Red Ryder collectibles.

## Red Ryder BB Guns

Red Ryder BB guns marked No. 111   $100
  Model 40, with copper plated
    barrel bands and iron cocking lever.

## Old BB Guns & Cap Pistols

| | |
|---|---|
| Daisy BB guns with wire stocks | $500 |
| BB guns marked Bulls Eye | 500 |
| Cast iron BB guns marked Columbian | 300 |
| BB guns marked Cycloid | 400 |
| BB guns marked Cyclone | 400 |
| BB guns marked Atlas | 300 |
| BB guns marked Matchless | 300 |
| BB guns marked Magic | 250 |
| BB guns marked Bijou | 250 |
| BB guns marked General Custer | 300 |
| BB guns marked Dewey or Crescent | 300 |
| BB guns marked Globe | 300 |
| BB guns marked Warrior | 300 |
| BB guns marked Hexagon | 300 |
| BB guns marked Remington | 300 |
| BB guns marked Heilprin | 200 |
| BB guns marked Sterling | 200 |
| BB guns mrkd American ToolWorks | 125 |
| BB guns marked American Dart Rifle | 100 |
| BB guns marked Wyandotte | 75 |
| BB guns marked Upton | 50 |

## Cap Pistols

Will pay for the following cast iron cap pistols in good to mint condition. Higher rewards for pieces in the orginal box.

| | |
|---|---|
| Cap pistols marked Roy Rogers | $450 |
| Cap pistols marked Long Tom | 300 |
| Cap pistols marked American | 200 |
| Cap pistols marked Big Horn | 150 |
| Cap pistols marked Gene Autry | 100 |
| Cap pistols marked Lone Ranger | 150 |

**Substantial rewards** for other cast iron, Western style cap pistols.

*Cast Iron cap pistols by Kilgore. Top left: "Long Tom," $300. Top Right: "Roy Rogers," $450. Center: "American," $200. Bottom Left & Right: "Big Horn." $150. Premium prices for guns in mint condition, and even more for guns in original box.*

*Daisy Military Guns. No. 40 & No. 140. Both came with sling & No. 40 came with detachable bayonet. $100-150 for BB gun. $100-150 for bayonet.*

*Early Daisys. All were originally nickel plated. Most are break action & have cast metal frame or trigger guards. A few have a top cocking lever. Some have wire stocks. $75-500 depending on model and condition.*

*Daisy Red Ryder, No. 111 model 40. With cast iron cocking levers. $75-100. Premium prices for guns with copper plated barrel bands and/or color lithographed original boxes.*

*"1000 Shot Daisy" or "500 Shot Daisy." Have 1901 & 1904 patent numbers. No model numbers. $150-350 depending on condition. Guns are nickel plated.*

*Daisy Buzz Barton guns. $50-75 for blued guns with oval stock label or brand. $75-150 for nickel plated guns with star stock brand. Guns must have rear sight tube & elevated front sight as shown to command full price.*

*Trombone pumps by Daisy or King. Marked "King No. 5 Pump Gun," "Daisy No. 105 Junior Pump Gun," "Daisy No. 107 Buck Jones" or "Ranger Pump Gun, Sear Roebuck & Co." $75-150 depending on model and condition. Daisy No. 25's are not included in this group.*

---

**Prices Paid by:**   Jim Buskirk
                    3009 Oleander Avenue
                    San Marcos, CA  92069         (619) 599-1054

# Pop Culture & Nostalgia

Ted Hake established Hake's Americana in 1967 and today the firm is America's leading mail and telephone bid auction house specializing in nostalgia and popular culture collectibles. Each year Hake's buys and sells 20,000 one of a kind collectibles. Hundreds of thousands of dollars are spent annually to purchase material in over 100 different categories to supply the thousands of worldwide customers who subscribe to five annual auctions. As Hake's has an exclusive worldwide clientele, we pay a high percentage of our anticipated retail to ensure a constant supply of quality collectibles for our customers.

---

### Pin-Back Buttons: Political and Non-Politcal.

Our personal favorite for over 30 years. We buy buttons that relate to every category. Defects like stain, scratches and splits greatly reduce value. Here are specific offers assuming no damage whatsoever. Send photocopies.

#### Political

| | |
|---|---|
| Pre-1896 lapel badges showing candidates on tin or cardboard photos | usually $100+ |
| McKinley & Hobart on bicycle | 3,000 |
| McKinley showing factory & dinner pail | 1,500 |
| McKinley or Bryan on hobby horse | 2,500 |
| McKinley or Bryan "Eclipse" buttons | 500+ |
| Teddy Roosevelt shown with Fairbanks | usually 50+ |
| Teddy Roosevelt shown with Johnson | 1,000 |
| James Cox 1920 picture buttons | any 100+ |
| Cox and Franklin Roosevelt BOTH PICTURED | 10,000 |
| Truman picture on 8-ball design | 4,000 |
| Most pre-1932 picture buttons | at least 15 |
| Votes for women & other political causes | 10 |

#### Non-Political

| | |
|---|---|
| Product advertising with pictures, pre 1920 | usually $10 |
| Farm equipment with pictures | usually 20 |
| Mickey Mouse or Donald Duck 1930s | usually 75 |
| Elvis Presley 1950s fan club | 100 |
| Cowboys – Tom Mix, Hoppy, Roy, Gene | usually 10 |
| Santa Claus 1930s or earlier | usually 35 |
| Lindbergh & early aviation | usually 15 |
| Wonder Woman 1940s | 500 |
| Flash or U.S. Jones 1940s | ea. 500 |
| Yellow Kid numbered series | ea. 20 |
| Kellogg's Pep comic characters | ea. 5 |
| Thousands of others - send photocopies | |

## WANTED ITEMS

**Advertising:** Ad figures representing Speedy Alka-Seltzer $150, Mr. Peanut wood jointed $100, Reddy Kilowatt $75+, Charlie The Tuna $15, hundreds of others. Also paper or objects from early years of famous American Companies.

**Artist:** From $10 for simple items to $1,000+ for original art by artists such as Disney, Vernon Grant, George Herriman, Winsor McCay, Maxfield Parrish, Richard Outcault and other comic character artists.

**Autographs:** Letters or signed photos of famous people like Marilyn Monroe $2,000, John Kennedy $1,000, Walt Disney $1,000 and hundreds of others.

**Aviation:** About anything from 1940s or earlier for real or toy airplanes or airships. World War II I.D. models $25+, Lindbergh toys or games $50+, Zeppelin souvenirs$ 25+

**Baseball:** Any World Series or All-Star items like programs or press pins, up to $1,000+ for early items, Hartland 1960s plastic figures $75+, bobbing head 1960s figures $25+. Nearly anything 1960s or earlier has some value.

**Beatles:** Any character merchandise from the 1960s such as toy guitar $150, record cases $75, lunch box 100+, also Yellow Submarine. Gum cards not wanted.

**Bicycles:** Lapel studs or buttons from 1900 era, each $5, League of American Wheelmen items $20+, medals for 1900 era meetings or races $25+, high wheel items, most $50+.

**Big Little Books:** All titles, for excellent condition $10.

**Black Americana:** Mechanical toys, most $100+, salt and pepper sets, most $20+, Martin Luther King signed photo $400.

**Boy Scouts:** Large calendars pre-1950 $25, most pinback buttons pre-1950 $10, many other items.

**Boxing:** Joe Louis clock or lamp $100, pre-1930s cards, each $3, famous fight program $20+.

**Captain Action:** Boxed figures or accessories $100+, loose figures $75, complete outfits $50+.

**Cars:** 1960s or earlier promotional toy models, most $50, 1930s or earlier wind-ups most $100+.

**Cels:** Most Disney 1950-60 $100+. Disney 1940s most $500+, also many non-Disney $100+.

**Comic Characters:** Almost anything depicting comic or cartoon characters from the 1970s or earlier is of interest. Prices range from $3 for Flintstone jelly glasses to $2,000 for Mickey Mouse 1930s radio.

**Cowboys:** All items wanted for movie and TV cowboys. Most popular are Tom Mix, Hopalong Cassidy, Roy Rogers. Prices range from $400 for Tom Mix movie posters to $75 for Bonanza lunch boxes.

**Cracker Jack:** Any pre-1950 paper or metal item, each $10. Not wanted–plastic items or presidential coins. Items must have company name or "C.J. Co."

**Dixie Lids:** Any clean condition lid, at least $3. Any 8 x 10" premium picture $5+.

**Dolls:** Any related to specific character or real person: Elvis 1950s $1,000, Mickey or Minnie Mouse 1930s $200+, Roy Rogers or Hopalong Cassidy $250, many others $100+.

**Elvis:** All items from 1956-60s era. Gum cards $3 each, toy guitar $250, wallet $100, photo ring $100, much more.

**Expositions:** Most pre 1970 exposition material is collected. Many items are in $5-10 range. Exception 1939 radio, $400, 1933 lamp $100, many others $25+.

**Fire:** Most pinback buttons or ribbon badges, pre 1930, $5-10.

**GI Joe:** Only want 1960-1970s large size figures and accessories. Boxed American soldiers $100+, Foreign soldiers $200+, most unboxed figures $50-100, boxed or packaged accessories, many $100+. Loose pieces also purchased.

**Gum Cards:** All non-baseball cards from 1960s and earlier. Many sets $100+, many individual cards $2 each.

**Lunch Boxes:** Metal boxes wanted from 1960s and earlier. Mickey Mouse 1930s $500, Underdog $500, Jetsons $400, Paladin $200, many others $100+.

**Mirrors:** Celluloid covered advertising pocket mirrors usually 2 1/2" or smaller. Colorful pictures add value. Most $25, rarities $100+.

**Movies:** Posters, lobby cards, games, figural objects related to pre-1950 famous stars and movies. Wizard of Oz or Gone With The Wind 1939 buttons, each $100, posters for original release of classic films, many $500+.

**Pin-Ups:** Calendars by Varga $50, card decks, many $25+, Playboy first issue $500, paper items by Elvgren or Moran, many $ 10+.

**Presidential Campaigns:** Snuff boxes, $500+, ribbons with portraits, most $75+, cardboard or tintype photo badges, most $100+, pin-back buttons with pictures 1896-1932, $15 each. All types of pre-1964 material wanted.

**Pulp Magazines:** $10-15 for titles like Weird Tales, Doc Savage, G-8, The Spider, The Shadow, Spicy Detective, many others.

**Radio & Cereal Premiums:** Wanted all giveaways like rings, decoders, maps, club manuals for shows like Tom Mix, Orphan Annie, Dick Tracy, The Shadow, Green Hornet, Tarzan, Space Patrol, Buck Rogers, Howdy Doody and many more. Buck Rogers knife $500, Lone Ranger 6-Gun ring $50, Orphan Annie decoder $20, Captain Marvel statuette $3,000, Superman 1940s contest ring $5,000+, hundreds more worth $25-500.

**Robots:** Most from 1960s or earlier such as Lost In Space $200, Mr. Atomic $5,000, many $200+.

**Television:** Most items related to shows from 1948 - early 1970s. First TV Guide $300, Howdy Doody wood doll $250, Hopalong Cassidy cap gun $100, most board games pre-1970, $20+, most lunch boxes pre-1970 $35, dolls, many $75+, much more.

**Toys:** All types from 1960s and earlier. Comic character windups 1930s, most $200+, battery toys 1960s boxed, many $100+, Marx playsets complete, many $200+, Aurora monster or character model kits 1960s unbuilt, many $100+, much more.

**World War** II: Homefront or anti-axis items, Douglas MacArthur, Remember Pearl Harbor, V for Victory. Prefer figural objects but much paper (and Posters) also of interest. Paying $1,000 each for arcade games with anti-axis themes.

---

**Prices for undamaged items paid by:**

Hake's Americana & Collectibles
POB 1444TH
York, PA  17405          (717) 848-1333 M-F  10-5 Eastern

All inquiries answered. Send photos or photo copies. From those we can usually make a tentative offer. Note any defects. If interested, we will provide shipping instructions. Payment is made immediately upon receipt of item, subject to revision only if the item's condition is less than anticipated when the tentative offer was made.

---

# Political & Other Buttons

## HAKE'S SAMPLE BUYING PRICES
### (All Values Assume Excellent Condition)

**LINCOLN (1860-1864)**
Tin Photo (front only) $200+
Tin Photo (both sides) $300+
Lincoln and VP both on front
$1000+
Lincoln cardboard photo
lapel badge $200+
Lincoln Ribbons: w/portrait
$500; no portrait $300

**TEDDY ROOSEVELT**
Hugged by Uncle Sam - $2500
Uncle Sam Holding Scales - $4500
TR "Equality" Buttons - $2500+
Colorful 7/8" or larger
picture buttons $20+

**COX AND FDR**
Both pictured
$6500
(more for scarcer designs)

---

**SEND A PHOTOCOPY OF YOUR SMALL COLLECTIBLES. THIS IS A TINY SAMPLING OF 1000's OF ITEMS WE WANT TO PURCHASE. ASK FOR OUR FREE WANT LIST. THANK YOU.**

---

**TRUMAN**
For Judge $1000
For Senator $150
8-Ball Design $4000
Pictured w/Barkley $100+

**FARM EQUIPMENT**
Avery - $75
Steam Tractors - most $75
Plows, etc. - most $35

**GUNPOWDER**
Spencer Oval - $125
Other Marksmen - $75
Remington Bears - $85
Most others w/pictures - $40

**POCKET MIRRORS**
Berry Varnishes - oval - $200
Berry Varnishes - round - $75
Most multicolor product ads - $50

**YELLOW KID**
Buttons #1 -39 @ $20
Buttons #40 - 89 @ $30
Buttons #90 - 94 @ $75
Buttons #101 - 160 @ $30

**DONALD DUCK**
"Wanna Fight"
$400

**"KELLOGG'S PEP"**
on reverse
Felix or Phantom $30
other characters $5
Military Insignia $3
Airplanes $45

**OPERATOR 5 RING**
$4000

**CAPT. MIDNIGHT**
Mystic Sun God Ring
$750

Hake's Americana pays a high percentage of retail value to acquire small collectibles. Ted Hake established his mail bid auction house in 1967 and has a constant need to purchase items for his five annual auctions. Ted buys much more than small collectibles (see his two-page listing under Pop Culture & Nostalgia), but pin-back buttons and other small collectibles remain his favorite, even after 30 years. With a nationwide clientele of advanced collectors as customers, Hake's buying prices usually exceed what local dealers or collectors will pay. Send photocopies for a quick preliminary offer.

# POLITICAL

### Pre-1896

BROOCHES—usually glass with image of W.H. Harrison or log cabin. $200+

MEDALETS—usually w/image of candidate and "For President" common $10-$25; rarities $100+

RIBBONS—most w/portrait $50-$150; varieties with portrait for Jackson, Van Buren, Polk, Cass, Lincoln-$500+

LAPEL BADGES—most with cardboard photos $100; with tin type photo usually $200. More for rarities.

ALSO WANT bandannas, posters, snuff boxes, figural items, canes, torches, etc. 1800s-1968

### 1896 and Later

CELLULOID BUTTONS—common designs w/picture of presidential candidate pre-1932, most at least $15

JUGATE BUTTONS—picture both running mates. Common varieties 1896-1960 most $15-30, but many $100-200 and $1000+

LITHOGRAPHED TIN BUTTONS—usually common particularly if no pictures but some 1930s era with both pictures can be $100+

CAUSE BUTTONS—needed for third parties, early labor leaders, civil rights, Votes for Women, anti-Viet Nam War. Most $15-$25

## ADVERTISING

PRODUCT BUTTONS—pre 1930 with pictures usually $10 each, cars with pictures $30+, most gun powder $40+, most farm equipment $20+

HUNTING & FISHING LICENSES—want pre-1950. Common "Resident" examples at least $10. More for non-resident or southern and western states.

POCKET MIRRORS & DEXTERITY PUZZLES—most common examples around $15 but with early, full color designs many $100+

SANTA CLAUS BUTTONS—full color, celluloid covered from 1930s and earlier usually $35+

TRANSPORTATION 1896-1930s—want those relating to cars, aviation, motorcycles, bicycles etc. Many $5-$15 and $100+ for rarities

GAS & OIL RELATED—need buttons, giveaways, can banks most $10-$25. Paying $100 for certain service station or taxi hat or uniform metal badges.

MISCELLANEOUS—buttons, clickers, tops, watch fobs, etc. relating to Cracker Jack, Scouts, Marbles, Sports, World's Fairs & Wars.

## COMIC RELATED

PIN-BACK BUTTONS—picturing comic characters, cowboys, movie and TV personalities are wanted from all eras. Most are in $5-$25 range but many higher values. Paying $200 for 1930s Wizard or Oz buttons and $500 for 1930s Buck Rogers & Flash Gordon movie serial club buttons.

CLUB BADGES—usually brass, for kid's clubs such as The Lone Ranger, Orphan Annie, Tom Mix, Dick Tracy and other comic or radio characters. Most $25-$75 but as much as $350 for Capt. America and Tarzan.

CHARACTER RINGS—kid's premiums from radio shows or cereal. 100s in the $25-$200 range and well over $2000 for "Superman of America Members," Orphan Annie with moveable brass pieces on top, The Spider red & black enamel top, Cisco Kid Secret Compartment, Valric the Viking.

Also want 1960s-1970s plastic rings. Most $5-$25 but $200 for Quisp or Quake cereal rings.

CHARACTER PREMIUMS—of all kinds are sought. Decoders, club manuals, maps, etc. Nearly anything for any character.

---

### Contact: Ted Hake

P.O. Box 1444TH ● York, PA 17405-1444 ● 717-848-1333 (M-F/10-5 Eastern)

For an immediate offer send items by insured mail in a box. For a tentative offer send photocopies. Defects like stain, scratches and splits can only be determined by examining the items to make an offer fair to us and you. Payment is made immediately upon your acceptance of our offer. Items are returned at our expense if you pass on our offer. Thank you for considering Hake's.

# Barbie Dolls

## BARBIE & FAMILY

NUMBER ONE: Brunette, retouched red lips, near mint in box with swimsuit, shoes, glasses, hoop earrings, number one booklet and box.    1200-1500

NUMBER TWO: Blonde, sumptuous red lips, long thick hair, pinky pink skin, beautiful complexion, mint in box with everything.    1500-2000

NUMBER THREE: Blonde, blue eye liner, red lips, otherwise excellent condition    150-200

NUMBER THREE: Blonde, blue eye liner, all original in her black and white swimsuit, excellent condition.    125-150

NUMBER FOUR: Brunette, red lips & long hair. Swimsuit, pretty face, excellent condition.    100-150

NUMBER FIVE: Redhead, red lips, gorgeous face, Swimsuit, excellent condition.    75-100

NUMBER FIVE: Blonde, gorgeous aqua eyes, red lips, nude, smashing, excellent condition.    50-75

NUMBER SIX: Ash blonde, coral lips, attractively pretty face and body, excellent condition.    50-75

BUBBLE CUT: Black hair, red lips, mint in box complete    150-175

BUBBLE CUT: Black hair, red lips, nude, near mint.    30-50

BUBBLE CUT: Red hair, red lips, nude, beautiful face, full hair, excellent condition.    30-50

BUBBLE CUT: Redhead, large watermelon lips, nude, excellent condition.    40-50

BUBBLE CUT: Rare! Brownette color, red lips, black and white swimsuit, mint.    200-250

SWIRL: Blonde, pale orange lips, mint in box with everything (even cheek blush).    200-250

SWIRL: Blonde, retouched coral lips, nude, excellent condition.    50-75

FASHION QUEEN: Blue band, gold and white striped swimsuit, wig stand and 3 wigs, no turban, otherwise excellent condition.    95

MISS BARBIE: 23 wigs with wig stand, swimsuit, hat, orange band, tiny melt mark, mint.    150-175

BENDABLE LEG AMERICAN GIRL: Redhead, pale orange lips, never removed from box.    400

BENDABLE LEG AMERICAN GIRL: redhead, pale orange lips with really curly hair at the side, mint in box.    350

BENDABLE LEG AMERICAN GIRL: blonde hair, dark orange lips, fabulous mint in box    400

SIDE PART: Doll with black silver hair and original head band, original thread still in hair; color magic face with deep red lips and rosy cheeks and gorgeous eye shadow. Original mint swimsuit, rare and VHTF    1500

BENDABLE LEG AMERICAN GIRL: Pale blonde, cantaloupe lips, nude, near mint.    200-250

BENDABLE LEG AMERICAN GIRL: Brunette, red lips, slight hair cut, excellent condition.    100-125

BENDABLE LEG AMERICAN GIRL: Long golden cinnamon hair, coral lips, original swimsuit, near mint    200-300

COLOR MAGIC: Lemon blonde, original hair band & barrette, swimsuit & shoes, deep geranium lavish lips, minty mint.    200-250

HAIR FAIR: Brunette head on standard body, long lashes, rosy cheeks, excellent condition near mint.    30-40

HAIR FAIR: Blonde on standard body, excellent condition    20-30

TWIST AND TURN: Platinum, 1967, original top and bottom, no belt, original bow, near mint/mint.    50-60

TALKING BARBIE: Dark, dark brunette, 1969, original swimsuit in original box, mint in box.    75-100

LIVING BARBIE: Red hair, with the hard to find centered eyes and long eye lashes In polka dot swim suit.    30-40

NEW BARBIE WITH GROWIN' PRETTY HAIR: Never removed from box but box is shop worn.    60-80

MONTGOMERY WARDS BARBIE: Mint in box with wrist tag. This is the brown cardboard Ward's box.    250-350

QUICK CURL BARBIE: Original dress, brush, comb & curler, mint.    10

DELUXE QUICK CURL BARBIE: In original outfit and shawl, mint.    10

STRAIGHT LEG MIDGE: Redhead or brunette, with wrist tag and original liner, never removed from box, pristine mint    95

STRAIGHT LEG MIDGE: Blonde, mint in box with original swimsuit, booklet and shoes, replaced liner.    50-60

BENDABLE LEG MIDGE: Blonde, original swimsuit & hair band, left knee does not click, otherwise near mint.    100-125

NEW TALKING STACEY: Red hair, mint in box with reattached wrist tag and 2-piece striped swimsuit, mint in box.    75-100

TALKING STACEY: Long red hair, in the cardboard and celloed box, 2-piece striped swimsuit, never removed from box.    150-175

### 1976

BEAUTIFUL BRIDE: European version, box worn.    30-40

BEAUTIFUL BRIDE: Made in Korea, box worn.    30-40

**1974** GOLD MEDAL KEN SKIER    50

**1970** THE SUN SET MALIBU KEN    25

### Barbie Older Fashions - Never Removed From Box

| | |
|---|---|
| COMMUTER SET: With #1 booklet | 500 |
| RED FLARE | 40-50 |
| DINNER AT 8 | 40-80 |
| WINTER HOLIDAY | 40-60 |
| BUSY GAL | 250 |
| AMERICAN AIRLINE STEWARDESS | 90 |
| OPEN ROAD | 100-125 |
| SINGING IN THE SHOWER | 50-60 |
| BALLERINA | 75-90 |
| JUNIOR DESIGNER | 100-150 |
| SKATER'S WALTZ | 100-125 |
| MATINEE FASHION: With spikes | 200-225 |
| GOLD 'N GLAMOUR: With spikes | 400-500 |

### Barbie Older Fashions – No Boxes

IT'S COLD OUTSIDE: In brown, complete, near mint, in red, complete and mint.    20-25

BARBIE IN JAPAN: complete mint with booklet    100-110

CINDERELLA: Complete, near mint with booklet.    100-110

ARABIAN NIGHTS: No booklet, otherwise complete and mint.    50-75

LITTLE RED RIDING HOOD: No booklet, otherwise complete and near mint/mint.    100-125

CANDY STRIPER VOLUNTEER: Complete and near mint/mint.    125-150

GOLDEN GIRL: Complete and near mint.    20-25

GARDEN PARTY: Complete, excellent condition    15-20

AFTER FIVE: Complete and excellent condition    15-20

SORORITY MEETING: Complete, excellent condition, near mint.    25-30

### Barbie Glamour Group:

Very rare Braniff serving dress, near mint/mint.    50-75

Very rare Braniff boarding outfit, no helmet, otherwise complete, near mint/mint    125-175

Boots, mint    30-50

### Barbie Pack - Mint on Card

BARBIE DRESS MAKERS    10

SHOE WARDROBE: Mint on card, page 78 Eames    70

PERFECT BEGINNINGS: Hot pink flowered panties & bra with sheer hot pink ruffled half slip, talc & puff    25

WHITE & BLACK PRINT BLOUSE: With red purse    10

PINK SATIN BOLERO JACKET AND HAT    25

WHITE SATIN LONG SKIRT: With silver glitter heels    35

FASHION FEET    30

---

**Prices Paid by:**    Marl Davidson
10301 Braden Run
Bradenton, FL 34202

(941) 751-6275
marlbe@aol.com

---

# Beatles Memorabilia

Collectors usually want Beatles items produced during the group's existence, 1960-1970. Items produced after 1970 are of little value or interest. Prices quoted are for items in complete, clean condition. Although *all* original items have some value, only a few of the most desireable pieces are listed below.

### Toys, games & crafts

| | |
|---|---|
| Rubber ball | $300 |
| Bubblebath containers | 60 |
| Colorforms | 350 |
| 5" rubber/plastic dolls (set) | 225 |
| 8" bobbin head dolls in box | 400 |
| 14" bobbin head dolls (each) | 700 |
| Flip Your Wig game | 80 |
| Halloween costumes (boxed) | 350 |
| Megaphone | 300 |
| Model kits (unbuilt) | 200 |
| Paint by number kits | 400 |
| Skateboard | 1,000 |

### Musical Instruments

| | |
|---|---|
| Banjo & bongos | $1000 each |
| Drum | 800 |
| Guitars (toy) | 200-1000 each |
| Harmonica in box | 100 |

*Above:*
Coloring book
store display
without books

*Right:*
Maestro
Beatleist
guitar

$500

$450

### Miscellaneous Items

| | |
|---|---|
| Record player | $1,800 |
| Concert tickets (unused) | up to 500 |
| Concert tickets stubs | up to 150 |
| Jewelry | 50 |
| Pennants | 60 |
| Drinking glasses | 80 |
| Promotional posters | 300 |
| Gum cards | 60¢ each |
| Hairspray can | 500 |

### Records

| | |
|---|---|
| Promotional LPs & 45s | up to $1000 |
| Can't Buy Me Love sleeve | 200+ |
| Please Please Me sleeve | 100+ |
| Others | up to 100 |
| Original LPs (unopened) | 300+ |

### Yellow Submarine items

| | |
|---|---|
| Alarm clock | $500 |
| Banks | 200 ea. |
| Dimensionals | 250 ea. |
| Goebel figurines | 700 ea. |
| Halloween costumes | 350 |
| Clothes hangers | 75 ea. |
| Lunch box | 200 |
| Puzzles | 50-80 ea. |
| Wristwatch | 800 |

Many other items are wanted. Autographs with good documentation considered. These are just a few of many items produced bearing the likeness of the greatest group of all time, the Beatles!

---

**Prices Paid by:** Jeff Augsburger
The Beatles Mobile Museum
507 Normal Avenue
Normal, IL 61671

(309) 452-9376
Fax (309) 454-2351
beatles@dave-world.net

Sellers should provide description of items, include condition, color, identifying marks. Photos are helpful and will be returned. Please include phone or fax number. Serious collector for over 20 years!

# GI Joe™ Action Figures

I'll buy accessories, figures, uniforms and vehicles. I prefer items made between 1964-69, but I will consider anything in good condition whether it is boxed, carded or loose.

I also will buy calendars, child-sized toys, clothing, coloring books, department store catalogs and advertising materials, games, industry periodicals, inflatables, jewelry, novelties, old newspaper & magazine ads, old television commercials on film, paper dolls, puzzles, salesman catalogs & invoices, postcards, toy store catalogs & invoices and watches.

I am searching for any **historically significant material** related to GIJoe® action figures including photographs and home movies of children playing with GIJoe® (or other 1960's era toys). I would love to hear from artists, child actors, designers, factory workers, models, photographers, salesman or anyone else who either worked for **HASBRO®**, then **HASSENFELD BROTHERS**, or the GIJoe® toy industry in the 1960's. Old GIJoe® store stock has been found in barns used for storage, basements, five & dime stores, greeting card shops, hobby shops, pharmacies, px stores, tobacco stores, toy stores and old Western Auto stores. I will pay **finders fees** for leads on old warehouse stock. Especially looking for artwork, prototypes and salesman samples, as well as, store displays. I will pay up to **$10,000** for a completely filled 1964 store display rack.

Please send photographs or a videotape of your collection. Note any defects. All inquiries answered if you include an SASE. If interested, I will supply shipping instructions. I **do not** cherry pick your best items and leave you the junk. I will only buy complete collections. Payment is made upon receipt of item(s).

Joe purchases for both his personal collection and resale. He is the publisher and editor of **Headquarters Quarterly™ Magazine**, also he runs the GIJOE® WWW FAN CLUB™ on the Internet.

## Follow These Easy Steps to Sort the Good from the Bad

The highest prices are paid for GIJoe® figures that have:
- Painted heads/hair with no scratches;
- Stiff bodies with tight joints;
- Thick fully painted eyebrows;
- Clean pressed clothing.

Painted head dolls are worth more than fuzzy ones, and a 1967 nurse doll mint in her box could bring $2,000.

The least prices are paid for the GIJoe® figures that have:
- Painted heads/hair with scratches;
- Cracked bodies with loose joints;
- Eyebrows that are scratched or rubbed off;
- Dirty or torn clothing;
- Rusted or borken parts.

Don't clean, iron or wash anything. If you do, you will lower the value even more!

(Top) *Children's backyard patrol sets*
*Paying up to $100*

(Bottom) *Loose figures*
*Paying up to $100*

*Prototype [left]*
*Paying up to $2,000*

*Common [right]*
*Paying up to $200*

BOOTS

*Original package artwork*
*Paying up to $2,000*

*Nurse MIB*
*Paying up to $2,000*

**MEDIC ARM BANDS**

**Prices Paid by:** Joe Bodnarchuk
62 McKinley Avenue
Kenmore, NY 14217-2414`
(716) 873-0264    Fax (716) 873-0264    gijoe@bodnarchuk.com

# Pop Culture

## McDonalds

- $500.00 for McDonalds character fiberglass playground figures in fine or better condition.
- $100.00 or more for interior restaurant decorations that are character related. Also want bubble displays.
- $50.00 or more for early McDonalds promotional merchandise with the SLASH M logo. (Slash M logo has a line crossing through the M at an angle).
- Ronald McDonald Charleton comic books.
- Early McDonalds characters Speedy & Archie also wanted.

### Tim Burton's
## Nightmare Before Christmas

Toys, Dolls, Cookie Jars, Action Figures & Promotional items from the 1993 Disney Movie. Items in original packaging preferred. I am NOT looking for small 3 inch rubber figures, pencils, key chains, party favors or damaged items. Please call or E-Mail me with accurate descriptions.

## Peanuts Characters
### Snoopy, Charlie Brown, Lucy, Linus, Pig Pen & Shroder from before 1975

Paying $50.00 or more for most anything Ceramic or Plastic, especially music boxes, figural nodders, jointed figures and banks. All items must be in excellent condition.

| Prices Paid by: | Mark Blondy |
| --- | --- |
| | 1865 Beverly |
| | Sylvan Lake, MI 48320 |
| | (248) 640-4197  till 10pm Eastern    tradertime@aol.com |

# Pez Candy Items

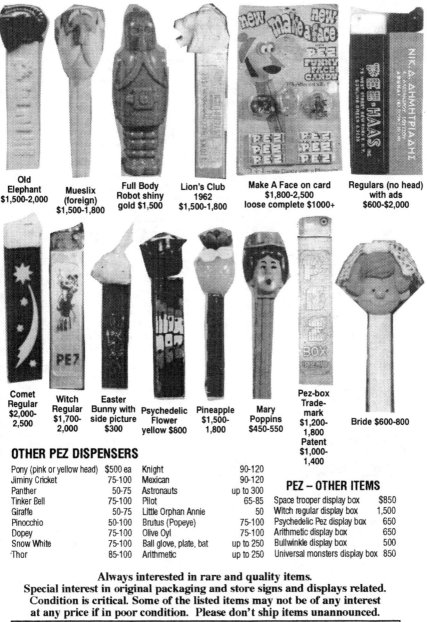

**Old Elephant** $1,500-2,000

**Mueslix (foreign)** $1,500-1,800

**Full Body Robot shiny gold** $1,500

**Lion's Club 1962** $1,500-1,800

**Make A Face on card** $1,800-2,500 **loose complete** $1000+

**Regulars (no head) with ads** $600-$2,000

**Comet Regular** $2,000-2,500

**Witch Regular** $1,700-2,000

**Easter Bunny with side picture** $300

**Psychedelic Flower yellow** $800

**Pineapple** $1,500-1,800

**Mary Poppins** $450-550

**Pez-box Trademark** $1,200-1,800 **Patent** $1,000-1,400

**Bride** $600-800

## OTHER PEZ DISPENSERS

| | | | | |
|---|---|---|---|---|
| Pony (pink or yellow head) | $500 ea | Knight | 90-120 | |
| Jiminy Cricket | 75-100 | Mexican | 90-120 | |
| Panther | 50-75 | Astronauts | up to 300 | |
| Tinker Bell | 75-100 | Pilot | 65-85 | |
| Giraffe | 50-75 | Little Orphan Annie | 50 | |
| Pinocchio | 50-100 | Brutus (Popeye) | 75-100 | |
| Dopey | 75-100 | Olive Oyl | 75-100 | |
| Snow White | 75-100 | Ball glove, plate, bat | up to 250 | |
| Thor | 85-100 | Arithmetic | up to 250 | |

## PEZ – OTHER ITEMS

| | |
|---|---|
| Space trooper display box | $850 |
| Witch regular display box | 1,500 |
| Psychedelic Pez display box | 650 |
| Arithmetic display box | 650 |
| Bullwinkle display box | 500 |
| Universal monsters display box | 850 |

**Always interested in rare and quality items.**
**Special interest in original packaging and store signs and displays related.**
**Condition is critical. Some of the listed items may not be of any interest**
**at any price if in poor condition. Please don't ship items unannounced.**

**Prices Paid by:** David Welch
2308 Clay Street or P.O. Box 714
Murphysboro, IL 62966
(618) 687-2282    Fax (618) 684-2243
Wrote: *Pictorial Guide to Plastic Candy Dispensers* (1991) & *Collecting PEZ* (1995)

# Pop Culture

**Note:** Prices for excellent to mint items with original package/box

### Pre-1930

| | |
|---|---|
| Winsor McKay's Gertie the Dinosaur poster | $25,000 |
| Yellow Kid in McFadden's Flats, 1897 | 2,500 |
| Little Sammy Sneeze, 1905 NY Herald | 1,000 |
| Little Nemo in Slumberland books 1906-9 | 1,000 ea |
| 'Little Nemo character figurines | 1,000-2,000 ea |

### 1930's

| | |
|---|---|
| Operator 5 ring (skull with "5") | $2,500-8,000 |
| Myles Salt Box, Tarzan cut-outs | 250 |
| Buck Rogers roller skates | 3,000 |
| Buck Rogers Daisy liquid helium pistol | 1,200 |
| Buck Rogers Chemical Lab, Gropper Co. | 500-1,000 |
| Lone Ranger Ice Cream comic book #1, 1939 | 500-2,000 |
| Donald Duck Autograph Hound movie poster | 4,000-6,000 |
| Disney's Mother Goose Goes to Hollywood movie poster | 3,000-5,000 |
| Buck Rogers Cut-Out Adventure Book, uncut | 2,000 |
| Mickey Mouse Book, 1930 Bibo & Lang | 1,500-3,000 |
| Mickey Mouse Waddle Book, DJ, unused | 3,500 |
| Betty Boop pocket watch | 2,000 |
| Mickey & Minnie Motorcycle, Germany tin | 10,000-20,000 |
| Wizard of Oz Waddle Book, DJ, unused | 4,000 |
| Big Little Mother Goose, Whitman 576 pgs. | 500 |
| Adventures of Dick Tracy Big Little Book #707 | 500 |
| King Kong Puzzle, RKO in envelope | 600-900 |
| Frankenstein, Dracula, Mummy movie posters | 5,000-100,000 |
| Tarzan Twins Big Little Book, softcover | 100-300 |
| Big Little Paint Book, #721, unused | 300 |
| Tom Mix 5" bisque figure | 500-2,000 |
| Horrors of War collectors set box | 3,000 |

*Jack Armstrong, Crocodile Whistle-$1,000*

### 1940s

| | |
|---|---|
| Superman cut-outs book, Saalfield 1940 | $300-400 |
| Crocodile Whistle, Jack Armstrong, unmarked | 1,000 |
| Robot Lilliput NP5357, boxed | 5,000-8,000 |
| Phantom Club member pin | 400-600 |
| Donald Duck ceramic pie bird | 200 |
| Capt Marvel family statues, R. W. Kerr, boxed | 1,000-3,000 ea |
| Wonder Woman Sensation comics pin | 500-1,000 |
| The Flash-Fastest Man Alive pin | 500-1,000 |
| Batman Mask-newspaper giveaway | 700-1,000 |
| Marvel Bunny Statue, boxed | 1,500-3,000 |
| Little Orphan Annie Altascope ring (has 3 moveable plates) "Pursuit Plane" | 3,000-10,000 |
| Little Orphan Annie "SG" magnifying ring | 800-2,000 |
| "Supermen of America Member" ring | 5,000-20,000K |
| Kix cereal box-Atomic bomb ring on front | 500-800 |

### 1950s

| | |
|---|---|
| Howdy Doody Band, Linemar | $1,500-3,000 |
| Howdy Doody Jack-In-the Box ring | 2,000 |
| Elvis Presley board game, 1956 | 500-800 |
| Elvis Presley guitar, 1956 | 600-1,000 |
| Elvis Presley shoes, 1956 | 500-800 |
| Hopalong Cassidy tuna can | 200 |
| Hopalong Cassidy roller skates | 400-600 |
| Hopalong Cassidy punch board | 250-350 |
| Hopalong Cassidy furniture | 500-1,000 ea |
| Machine Man robot | 10,000-20,000 |
| Jupiter robot | 10,000-20,000 |
| Herman & Katnip cookie jar | 3500 |
| Little Audrey cookie jar | 1,000-1,500 |
| Caspar the Ghost cookie jar | 400-600 |
| Robert the Robot on tractor, Ideal | 700-900 |
| Space Whale Ship "PioneOer PX-3" | 800 |
| Clarabell Clown delivery wagon, Linemar | 1,500-2,000 |
| Have Gun Will Travel holster set, Halco | 500 |
| Popeye & Mean Man, Linemar | 2,500-3,500 |
| Popeye juggling Olive Oyl, Linemar | 1,000-1,500 |
| Kelloggs Sugar Frosted Flakes cereal box, Katy Kangaroo & Superman Stereo Pix | 300-500 |
| Davy Crockett Indian Fighter Boots, Trimfoot | 225 |
| Circus Clown Robot In Mercedes, Japan | 800-1,200 |
| Roy Rogers remote control van, Linemar | 800 |
| "Try Your Skill" lucky crane | 500 |
| Space Fleet of the Future, Pyro | 300 |
| Lincoln Futura Car, ALPS Japan | 1,200-1,500 |
| Mechanical Ham N Sam, Linemar | 500-700 |
| Lassie trick trainer set | 200 |
| Hubley Atomic Disintegrator Gun | 300 |
| Mickey Mouse the Magician, windup | 2,500 |
| Roy Rogers moving picture lamp | 1,000 |
| Untouchables playset, Marx | 1,000 |
| Johnny Ringo playset, Marx | 800-1,200 |
| Speedy Alka Seltzer, 1957 P. W. Baston | 3,000 |
| Nabisco Spoonmen Shredded Wheat Jrs figures on base, P. W. Baston 1957 | 2,500 |
| Now's the Time for Jello, P. W. Baston figures | 200-300 |
| Swanson TV Dinner boxes | up to 100 |
| Superman Tank, battery, Linemar | 2,500 |
| Topple the Elephant lunch box, metal | 1,000 |
| Caine Mutiny, RCA soundtrack, LOC-1013 | 2,500 |

### 1960s

| | |
|---|---|
| Reddy Kilowatt vinyl bank with cloud | $400 |
| Gunsmoke playset, Marx | 1,000-1,500 |
| Flintstone miniature playset, Marx | 500 |
| Big Loo Robot, complete, Marx | 1,500 |
| Hamilton's Invaders playsets, Remco | 500 |
| Frankenstein Marx remote | 1,000 |
| windup | 500 |
| Lost in Space Roto Jet Gun, Mattel | 2,000 |
| Mad Mad Mad Scientist Lab | 1,000 |
| Superman-Supergirl push puppets, Kohner, set | 600 |
| Batman-Robin push puppets, Kohner, set | 1,000 |
| Matt Mason Space Diner vinyl lunch box | 1,200 |
| Choo Choo "Charlie & Friend", vinyl, Good N Plenty | 1,000 |

| | |
|---|---|
| Super Queens: Wonder Woman, Mera, | |
| Batgirl, Supergirl, Ideal | 1,000-3,000 ea |
| Capt Action Kool Pops box | 1,000 |
| Capt Action Halloween costume | 1,000 |
| Capt Action Spiderman outfit | 4,000 |
| Dr. Evil Disguises & Weapons set | 1,200 |
| Major Matt Mason's Scorpio Alien | 1,000 |
| Topps Wacky Packs Stickers-Cracked Animals | |
| #38, Ratz Crackers #32, unused | 300 ea |
| Banana Splits rings (4 diff.), Kelloggs | 300 ea |
| Funny Face drink stand | 500 |
| Creature From the Black Lagoon wallet | 300 |
| Creature From the Black Lagoon game | 500 |
| Famous Monsters photo print set | 1,000 |
| Green Hornet dashboard, Remco | 1,000 |
| Batman utility belt, Ideal 1966 | 1,500 |
| Batman Justice League playset, Ideal | 8,000 |
| Batman playset, Ideal | 5,000 |
| Batman Fact toothpaste with pamphlet | 500 |
| Marvel Superhero express train, Marx | 1,000 |
| Thor scooter, Marx | 500 |
| Munsters bowling set | 1,000 |
| Green Hornet inflatable raft | 500 |
| Man From Uncle Thrush rifle, Ideal | 1,000 |
| Voyage to Bottom of Sea "4 in 1 Gun Set", | |
| Remco | 1,500 |
| Voyage to Bottom of Sea Sub playset, Remco | 600 |
| Godzilla's Go-Cart, Aurora | 3,500 |
| King Kong's Thronester, Aurora | 3,500 |
| Lost in Space #420, Aurora | 1,200 |
| Banana Splits buggy, Aurora | 350 |
| Gigantic Frankenstein, Aurora | 1,000 |
| Ed Roth Robin Hood Fink model, Revell | 500 |
| Weird Ohs Helmet, Ideal | 350 |
| Beatles Yellow Sub figurines, Goebel | 1,200 ea |
| Beatles Nestles Quik can | 200 |
| Quisp Cereal figural ring | 750 |
| Quake Cereal World Globe ring | 600 |
| Star Trek Astro helmet/pistol set, Remco | 400 |
| Avengers Emma Peel doll | 500 |
| Jetsons Rosie the Robot windup | 1,000 |
| Jetsons Elroy in Rocket pull toy | 400 |
| Huckelberry Hound Ford Conv., 9" | 1,000 |
| Flintstones Stone Away piano, Jaymar | 500 |
| Addams Family tile puzzle | 200 |
| Johnny Quest Paint/Crayon by number | 200 ea |
| Outer Space Man, colorforms | 200 ea |
| Space Ghost tile puzzle | 100 |
| 3 Stooges photo print set | 500 |
| 3 Stooges book bag | 350 |
| 3 Stooges Jigsaw Puzzle, colorforms | 300 |

| | |
|---|---|
| Munsters wrist flashlight | 350 |
| Munsters Koach toy, AMT | 350 |
| Munsters target game, Ideal | 500 |
| Cragstan Mr. Atomic Robot | 7,000 |
| Twinkles bank | 300 |
| GI Joe Green Beret | 1,200 |
| GI Nurse, Hasbro | 1,500 |
| GI Joe Negro Adventurer #7905 | 1,200 |
| Liddle Kiddies Kafe vinyl Lunch Box, Mattel | 400 |
| Barbie & Francie's Snack Shack lunch box | 700 |
| Upsy Downsy Happy-Go-Round/Funny Feeder | 200 ea |
| Matt Mason vinyl wallet | 250 |
| Mars Attacks gum card box | 1,000 |
| Bubble Bath boxes, cartoon characters | 40-200 |
| Whistling Spooky Kooky Tree | 1,000 |
| Hometown Airport lunch box | 1,000 |
| Saint/Secret Agent soundtrack records | 150 ea |
| Weird Ohs stuffed dolls, Jee-Bee Toy | 500 ea |

## 1970s

| | |
|---|---|
| Star Wars Jawa 3 3/4" vinyl cape, Kenner | $700-1,000 |
| Star Wars Special Action Figure Sets | |
| (3-packs), Kenner | 400-700 ea |
| Star Wars Early Bird Pack, unopened, | |
| Kenner | 200-300 |
| Star Wars SSP Van Set, Vader vs. Heros, Kenner | |
| | 300-500 |
| Empire Strikes Back Tie bomber, Kenner | 350-450 |
| Tazmanian Devil, Dakin | 100-150 |
| Planet of the Apes drum set | 300-500 |
| Planet of the Apes bean bag chair | 150 |
| Partridge Family record cabinet | 200-300 |
| Partridge Family radio | 200-300 |
| Partridge Family school bus toy | 300-500 |
| Brady Bunch Kitty carry-all | 200 |
| KISS record player | 100-200 |
| KISS guitar | 100-200 |
| Aquaman vs. Great White Shark, Mego | 200 |
| Star Trek 1976 Aliens-Romulan, Andorian | 250 ea |
| TEEN TITANS, Mego | 200-300 ea |
| Ward's Exclusive Alter Ego-Clark Kent, | |
| Bruce Wayne, Dick Grayson, | |
| Peter Parker, Mego | 500-800 ea |
| Batman with removable hood, Mego | 225-350 |
| Robin with removable mask, Mego | 400-600 |
| AHI Official World Famous Supermonsters | 50-250 |
| Uncle Rolly car, Pillsbury | 200 |
| Alien figure, Kenner | 200 |
| Hot Wheels Sky Show 1970 | 450 |
| Josie & the Pussycats record, Capitol | 150 |
| Charlie's Angels Beauty hair care | 150 |

**Always interested in rare and quality items.**
**Special interest in original packaging and store signs and displays related.**
**Condition is critical. Some of the listed items may not be of any interest**
**at any price if in poor condition. Please don't ship items unannounced.**

| | |
|---|---|
| **Prices Paid by:** | David Welch |
| | 2308 Clay Street or P.O. Box 714 |
| | Murphysboro, IL 62966 |
| | (618) 687-2282    Fax (618) 684-2243 |

# Pop Culture & Nostalgia

As Time Goes By has been specializing in fine vintage memorabilia for over ten years with one of the largest selections in the Southwest. Here is a partial list of our wants. All items must be complete and in collectible condition.

**PERSONALITIES:** We buy all types of personality collectibles. This includes magazine covers (complete magazine), lobby cards, movie posters, stills, post cards, games, dolls, figures, etc.

| | |
|---|---|
| **MARILYN MONROE:** 1940's - 1970's | $10-300 |
| **Laff magazine 8/19/46 | 100-250 |
| **True Experiences mag. 9/47 | 50-150 |
| **BETTIE PAGE:** Late 1940's - Early 60's | |
| **LUCILLE BALL:** 1930's - 1980's | 5-300 |
| **JOHN WAYNE:** 1930's-1970's | 5-65 |
| **ROY ROGERS:** 1930's - Present | 5-500 |
| **GENE AUTRY:** 1930's - Present | 5-200 |
| **HOPALONG CASSIDY:** 1930's - 1970's | 5-500 |
| **BEATLES:** 1963 - 1975 | 5-300 |
| **ELVIS:** 1956 - 1977 | 5-200 |

Buck Rogers cartoon adventures $15-35

**COMIC RELATED:** We buy vintage comic related toys, figures, puzzles, books, records etc... super hero, Disney and Hanna-Barbera.

| | |
|---|---|
| **BETTY BOOP:** 1930's - 1950's | $20-200 |

**COWBOYS:** We buy any early items related to: Roy Rogers, Hoppy, Gene Autry, Tom Mix etc... Also, Comic/TV characters eg. Zorro, Davy Crocket, Bonanza, Gunsmoke etc... 5-500

**MAGAZINES:** We buy the following:

| | |
|---|---|
| **Life Magazines:** 1936-1972 | $1-40/ea |
| **First Issue | 30-50 |
| **Ben Hogan | 30-60 |
| **Burton/Taylor 4/13/62 w/BB Card | 60-100 |
| **Other Current Events:** Time/Newsweek/Post etc.. | |
| **Playboy:** 1953 - 60's | |
| **First Issue | 550-1,200 |
| **Sports Illustrated:** 1954-70's | |
| **First issue | 80-110 |
| **TV Guide:** Pre-national 1940's - 1980's | 1 - 300 |
| **Vintage movie magazines:** All types | |

*We also purchase: automotive, aviation, men's adventure, pulps, music related, Fortune, etc. Please Inquire.*

Detective Comics #27, $10,000-80,000

**COMIC BOOKS:** Prices paid are based on condition and rarity. We buy the following:

| | |
|---|---|
| **Golden Age:** 1930's-1940's | |
| **Detective #27 (as pictured) | $10,000-80,000 |
| **Marvel Comics #1 | 5,000-55,000 |
| **Silver Age:** 1960-1975 | |
| **Spiderman #1 | 600-12,000 |
| **Amazing Fantasy #15 | 1,000-18,000 |
| **Showcase #4 | 800-16,000 |
| **1940-50's Horror / Humor / War** | |
| **Mad #1 | 250-2,500 |
| **TV Related / Western:** 1950's-1970's | |

**Misc:** Cartoon related hard and soft cover books from 1900's-1930's (Cupples & Leon, McKay, Saalfield)

**NON-SPORTS CARDS:** We buy **ALL** high-grade cards from the 1880's - 1970's

| | |
|---|---|
| **Tobacco:** Allen & Ginter, Duke, Mecca | $2-20/ea |
| **Mecca Golf Early 1900's | 5-15 |
| **Gum:** 1930's - 1970's | |
| **1940's Superman and Lone Ranger | 5-75 |
| **Jets, Rockets, and Spacemen 1951 | 3-10 |
| **Mars Attacks | 5-15 |
| **Hoppy Foils 1950 | 20-50 |
| **Film Funnies w/movie star names 30's | 20-40 |
| **Premiums:** 1930's-1940's | |
| **Heinz Airplanes / Aviators 1930's | 5-10 |
| **Arm & Hammer:** All Series | .50 - 5.00 |
| **Misc:** Dixie Ice Cream lids, cartoon pin-backs | |

*Miles Davis on Blue Note #5022, $50-150*

**RECORDS:** We buy good records in all categories and formats (LP, 45, 45EP, 78, Compact 33 etc...)
   **JAZZ:** 1940's - 1960's (Blue Note,Prestige, Debut, Norgran, Clef, Verve, Riverside, Fantasy, Savoy, Bethlehem, Pacific Jazz, Emarcy, Contemporary, Dial, Mode, New Jazz, Tampa etc..    $ 5-200
   **ROCK / R&B:** 1950's-1960's    5-150
   **PERSONALITIES:** 1950's - 1960's - Pin-Ups etc...
   **BLUES / FOLK:** Through the 1960's    2-100
   **CLASSICAL:** 1957-early 60's Stereo -
   **RCA-LSC (Living Stereo)Shaded Dogs    2-25
   **RCA-LDS (Soria Series)    2-25
   **Mercury SR-Living Presence Stereo    2-25
   **Decca SXL-2000/6000 (British)    2-25
   **EXOTIC / LOUNGE:** Esquivel, Dick Schory etc...
   **Living Stereo / Stereo Action    2-15
   **MISC:** Picture Discs (Vogue), children's, comic, soul, advertisement, country (1950's)

**MOVIE & TV:** We buy vintage magazines, lobby cards, P/R photos, stills, posters, etc.

**SCOUTING:** We buy all Boy Scout and Girl Scout collectibles before 1970.
   **Magazines:** Boys Life, American Girl    $2-8
   **Books:** Early manuals    5-10
   **Equipment:** Badges, belts, jewelry etc...

**SPORTS:** We buy collectibles of the following sports celebrities:    $5-500
   **BASEBALL:** RUTH, GHERIG, COBB, MANTLE, DIMAGGIO, MARIS, WILLIAMS, MUSIAL
   **GOLF:** HOGAN, BOBBY JONES, BABE ZAHARIAS, NELSON, PALMER, NICKOLAS
   **We buy items related to the following sports: Baseball, Golf, Racing(All), Football, Basketball

**NORMAN ROCKWELL:** We buy Rockwell items from 1910's to 1970's. These items include: magazine covers (full magazines only), posters, calendars etc...
   Four Freedoms Posters    (large) $50
   (small) 30

**PIN-UP ART:** We buy the following:
   **Calendars:** Full calendars only by Varga, Petty, McPherson etc...    $20-75
   Mutoscope Arcade Cards:    1.50-5.00
   **Playing Cards:** Full Decks with Jokers    2-35
   **Pin-Up Magazines:** 1920's - 1960's (Complete)

**STAR WARS / STAR TREK:** We only buy vintage items including figures, cards, magazines, comic books, books, etc.    $3-40

**WALT DISNEY:** We buy Disney collectibles from the 1930's to the 1960's. This includes:
   **Books:** Pop-Up, Waddle, paint, linen, and hard and soft cover story books    $5-500
   **Misc:** Magazines, songsheets, toys, puzzles, calendars, games, cards, comics    2-200
   Mickey Mouse Magazine (Sum '35) #1 500-5,000

**WORLDS FAIRS:** We buy any literature or souvenirs during or about these expositions:
   **Columbian Expo:** 1893-1894
   Any Ferris Wheel items    $20-50
   China, Stevengraphs etc...
   **Century of Progress:** 1933 Chicago
   **Texas Centennial:** 1936
   **NY Worlds Fair:** 1939-1940

**\*Visit Our Web Page at:**
**http://www.astimegoesby.com/atgb**

**Prices Paid by:** As Time Goes By  (Stan, Enid and Jeff Gold)
7042 Dartbrook
Dallas, TX 75240
(972) 239-8621     Fax: (972) 239-9622     record@unicomp.net

# Toys

Toy collecting can be as simple and basic as you care to make it; but sooner or later many of us branch out and discover another type of toy that suddenly sparks our interest — and then another and another.

This listing is not meant to ehminate other toys. I appreciate your letter and/or collect call on *any* quality toy or collection (except dolls and trains). Perhaps we can both learn a little and help each other.  Prices are for toys in excellent condition.

## CAST IRON TOYS

### ARCADE. EARLY CAST IRON

| | |
|---|---:|
| Century of Progress buses, 5" - 14" | $250-600 |
| Taxis, Yellow or Checker, misc sizes | 700-1,400 |
| Ford Century of Progress 7" | 1,500 |
| Greyhound "Great Lakes Ex. 11" | 700 |
| Greyhound "Great Lakes Ex. 6 3/4" | 300 |
| International trucks, 1930's | 600-1,500 |
| Reo Coupe, No. 1247, 1931 | Call Me |
| Texas Centenial bus 10 3/4" | 1,200-1,500 |
| White Tank Truck 14", 1930 | 1,300 |
| Arcade Road Signs | 15-20 each |
| Arcade Garage | 200+ |
| Arcade Furniture | 50-200 |
| Arcade Tools | 5 |
| Arcade Weapons | 5 |
| Andy Gump Car with crank, license plate, Andy in blue suit, white shirt | 3,000 |
| Andy Gump Car, blue suit, white shirt | 2,700 |

Andy Gump car (Andy nickel plated)  $2,500

### HUBLEY CAST IRON

| | |
|---|---:|
| Bell Telephone truck, complete, 1931 | $500 |
| Black & White cab, 1920's | 800 |
| Panama Digger 13", Mack | 900 |
| Racer 5", "1790" | 100 |
| Racer 9 1/2", lift hand, see motor | 1,200-1,500 |
| Coupe, rumble seat 11" | 240 |
| Ladder truck, 13 1/2" | 500 |
| "Coal" truck 13 1/2" | 750 |
| Motorcycle, Harley-D, civilian 6" | 500 |
| Motorcycle, Harley-D, policeman 6 1/2" | 500 |
| Motorcycle, Harley-D, police, sidecar, rider | 450 |
| Motorcycle, On/Off police 8 1/2" L | 800 |
| Motorcycle, "Parcel Post" 9 1/4" L | 1,500 |
| Motorcycle, 'U.S. Air Mail" | 1,000 |
| Motorcycle, '"Traffic Car" | 1,700 |
| Hubley horse drawn "Royal Circus" pieces | |
| Band Wagon 4 horses, 7 riders, 22" | 1,350 |
| Band Wagon 2 horses, 7 riders, 22 1/2" | 1,600 |
| Band Wagon 4 horses, 8 riders, 30" | 1,400 |
| Bear Wagon 2 horses, 15" | 400 |
| Farmer Van, head revolves, 16" | 2,000 |
| Giraffe cage, 27" | 4,200 |
| Rhino wagon, 16" | 1,200 |
| Tiger Cage and two tigers, 16" | 400 |

### COMIC CHARACTER

| | |
|---|---:|
| Felix the Cat on scooter | $400 |
| Flash Gordon rocket fighter ship, 12" | 400 |

Toonerville Trolley wind-up  $700

| | |
|---|---:|
| Buck Rogers rocket | 450 |
| Felix and Mice pull toy | 325 |
| Happy Hooligan in car | 1,300 |
| Happy Hooligan police patrol | 2,000 |
| Henry and his Brother | 1,000 |
| Hi Way Henry Jalopy | 2,100 |
| Mama Katzenjammer spanking kid | 1,000-3,000 |
| Olive Oyl on tricycle | 1,200 |
| Popeye on unicycle7 | 500 |
| Popeye spinach patrol | 900 |
| Popeye Puncher, floor bag | 525 |
| Popeye Puncher, overhead bag | 1,200 |
| Popeye - other wind-ups | 300-2,500 |
| Sight Seeing Auto No. 899 | 3,000-5,000 |
| Toonerville Trolley, lead | 200 |
| Toonerville Trolley, cast iron | 350 |
| Toonerville Trolley, 1 7/8" | 300 |
| Powerful Katrinka Lifting Jimmy | 1,500 |
| Other comic character wind-ups?  Please call. | |

### DISNEY

| | |
|---|---:|
| Mickey Mouse Ferris Wheel in box | $550 |
| Mickey Mouse Roller coaster in box | 475 |
| Mickey Mouse, Donald Duck figures | 25-300 |
| Mickey Mouse bank, cast iron | 750 |
| Mickey Mouse Lionel Set No. 1536 | 1,000 |
| Mickey Mouse jazz drummer, 4 3/4" | 850 |
| Mickey Mouse 12"  "Cowboy Mickey" | Call |
| Donald Duck duet in box | 550 |
| Donald Duck on Pluto, wind-up | 1,200 |
| Donald Duck pulled by Pluto | 1,400 |
| Dopey tin wind-up, Marx | 275 |
| Jiminy Cricket wind-up, 5 1/2" | 325 |

Disney toys could take up all the space available. If you have early fine condition items, call collect and we can talk about your item or collection.

### FISHER-PRICE

Fisher-Price toys from the 1930's and 40's in near mint condition? Please call.·   $400-1,000+

## MATCH BOX

Prices are for cars and trucks issued in 1950's and early 1960's, mint in their original box.

| | | |
|---|---|---|
| #2 | Green dumper | $20 |
| #3 | Cement mixer | 15 |
| #4 | Tractor | 20 |
| #4 | Motorcycle | 25 |
| #5 | London bus | 25 |
| #14 | Ambulance, grey wheels | 15 |
| #17 | Taxi | 30 |
| #19 | MG sports car | 30 |
| #21 | Coach | 25 |
| #21 | Milk Float | 18 |
| #25 | VW | 20 |
| #27 | Cadillac | 18 |
| #31 | St. Wagon | 25 |
| #32 | Jaguar | 20 |
| #33 | Ford Zephyr | 12 |
| #34 | VW Van | 20 |
| #36 | Scooter | 30 |
| #37 | Coca Cola | 35 |
| #39 | Pontiac | 20 |
| #41 | Jaguar | 30 |
| #44 | Rolls, blue | 25 |
| #53 | Aston Martin | 20 |
| #56 | Bus | 25 |
| #65 | Jaguar | 20 |
| #66 | Motorcycle | 45 |
| #70 | Ford | 18 |
| #74 | Canteen | 20 |
| #75 | T-Bird | 30 |

Lehman motor kutsche w/orig box   $600

## LEHMANN

Excellent condition - Add 20% if you have box

| | |
|---|---|
| Autobus | $1,200 |
| Baker and Sweep | 1,900 |
| Echo motorcycle | 1,200 |
| EPL dirigible | 600 |
| Li La | 900 |
| Mandarin | 1,200 |
| Naughty Boy | 475 |
| Onkel | 500 |
| "Rollo Chair" | 600 |
| Tut Tut | 700 |
| Walking Couple | 1,800 |
| Zig Zag | 1,000 |

## CHEIN

| | |
|---|---|
| Rocket Ride with box | 750 |
| Space Ride with box | 600 |

## TOOTSIETOY pre-WWII

If you have them for sale, please write   $25-150

## TONKA, SMITH-MILLER, METAL CRAFT & BUDDY-L

all made steel toys valued at $100 or more, with Buddy-L's up to $2,000+. Please call.

## COURTLAND MFG. (with box)

| | | |
|---|---|---|
| # 500 | Circus cart | $320 |
| #1200 | Trailer truck | 250 |
| #1300 | Ice cream truck | 125 |
| #1400 | Fire truck | 225 |
| #1600 | Dump truck | 200 |
| #2150 | Rescue squad | 200 |
| #2050 | Milk truck | 250 |
| #2400 | Tow truck | 200 |
| #3100 | Dump truck | 250 |
| #2000 | Gasoline truck | 225 |
| #6500 | Ice Cream scooter | 250 |
| #7500 | Police car | 200 |

## LOUIS MARX

Excellent condition. Add 20% for box.

| | |
|---|---|
| Busy Bridge | $400 |
| Charleston Trio | 500 |
| Ghee Whiz Auto Racer | 600 |
| George the Drummer | 120 |
| Merry Makers Band | 500-700 |
| "Police Patrol" with side car | 200 |
| "Police Siren" motorcycle | 300 |
| "Police Squad" motorcycle | 200 |
| Ring a Ling Circus | 600 |
| "Rookie Cop" with siren | 300 |
| Sparkling Soldier motorcycle | 300 |

## SCHUCO, TPS and UNIQUE ART

all made wonderful wind-up toys. Please call.

## BANKS

Evaluating an unseen bank is nearly impossible as many have been reproduced or "restored". I want early banks with 70% to 85% of original paint, no rust, no cracks, and no major faults. Please call.

| | |
|---|---|
| Acrobat | $2,500 |
| Boy robbing bird's nest | 3,700 |
| Cabin Bank | 375 |
| Chief Big Moon | 1,000 |
| Uncle Sam | 1200 |
| Magician | 2200 |
| Leap Frog | 1200 |
| Clown on Globe | 1500 |
| Stump speaker | 900 |
| Dentist | 3,000 |
| Darktown battery | 2,000 |

Speaking dog   $1,200

---

**Prices Paid by:**   James A. Conley
2758 Coventry Lane N.W.
Canton, OH  44708

(330) 477-7725
Fax  (330) 879-2950

# Marklin Toys & Trains

Marklin German metal trains were powered by windup motors, electricity and live steam, and come in various sizes ("gauges"). Values run from under $100 for common HO trains to $10,000 up for 1930's O or I gauge toys in excellent condition. Value plummets if cars have dents, paint loss, rust, broken or missing parts.

**MARKLIN**

Marklin also made train accessories (stations, lamps, bridges) as well as cars, trucks, military items (cannons, tanks, etc.), stationary steam plants and accessories (tools, Ferris wheels, motors), working toy kitchen equipment, and other toys. Most items are marked Marklin, Germany or with a Marklin emblem (illustrated). Some are unmarked. Early models were handpainted; later toys were lithoed on metal. I collect almost anything made by Marklin before 1956 in nice condition. The list of trains below shows catalog numbers (marked on some models), length, number of wheels, years manufactured, & price ranges for examples in good to like new condition. Variations in color and model numbers may affect values. **Track widths:** O gauge = 1 1/4"; I gauge = 1 3/4"; HO (OO) gauge = 5/8".

**Locomotives, Passenger and Freight Cars in gauges O and I bring the highest prices.**

| | |
|---|---|
| R1020, 1904-15, 4-wheel lok w/ 4-wheel tender, 10" black windup, O gauge | $300-$1,000 |
| AR1020, 1908-14, as above but American, w/ cowcatcher & bell, O gauge | 300-1,500 |
| R910, 1936-53, 4-whl lok w/ 4-whl tender, 12" black windup, O gauge | 75-200 |
| R12910, 1934-54, as above but 20-volt electric | 125-350 |
| E66/12920, 1935-54, 8-whl lok w/ 6-whl tender, 16" blk 20-V electric, O ga | 400-1,000 |
| HR66/12920, 1933-54, 12-whl lok w/ 8-whl tender,21" blk 20V elec, O ga | 1,000-4,000 |
| HR4020 or 4920, 1929-37, as above but live steam powered (also green) | 2,000-10,000 |
| HR66/12921, 1932-38, as above but I gauge, 39" 20V electric | 2,000-6,000 |
| CCS66/12920, 1933-40, 18" 12-wheel green lok, O ga "crocodile" | 5,000-15,000 |
| AK70/12920, 1936-38,'49, 14-whl lok w/ 12-whl tender, 24" 20V "Commodore Vanderbilt" & "New York Central" black w/ cowcatcher, O gauge | 4,000-13,000 |
| [2924] 1934-38, 12-whl dark green passenger car, 20" Pullman" | 1,000-3,000 |
| 19410, 1934-39 [1946-49?], green passenger car coach, 16" O ga, no interior | 300-1,000 |
| 19410 [G], 1934-39, as above but with fitted interior seating | 600-1,300 |
| 19420, as above, but red or blue diner, with or w/o interior seating | 300-2,000 |
| 19411, 19421, 19431, 1934-38, as above but 23" ga I | 500-2,400 |
| 19451, 19461, 19471, 1921-28, as above but 21" ga I | 500-2,400 |

**O and I gauges:**

**Stations, Lamps, Signals, Bridges, Cranes, etc.**

| | |
|---|---|
| Early large stations | up to $10,000 |
| Stations from the 1920's and '30's | 100-2,000 |
| Lamps (electric or oil-lighted) | 50-500+ |
| Simple bridges from the '30's | 100-300 |
| Elaborate pre-WWI bridges 24+" long | 1,000+ |

**Freight cars, 4 or 8-wheel, come in many types**

| | |
|---|---|
| Simple flat cars and gondolas | $20-50 |
| Oil tank cars | 50-1,000 |
| Beer cars marked w/ German beers | 150-1,000 |
| Hand ptd cars w/circus wagons | up to 10,000 |

**O and I gauge brown or green locomotives** with overhead pickups 1901-1954, clockwork or electric — $100-7,500

**HO gauge:**

| | |
|---|---|
| Locomotives, 5" - 12" long | 10-1,000 |
| (longer for 2-part and 3-part streamliners) | |
| Passenger cars | 5-500 |
| Freight cars | 2-200 |

Track & transformers are common with little value.

**NOTE: Do not clean or "fix" old toys!**

---

**Prices Paid by:** Ron Wiener
1650 Arch St. 22nd Flooor
Philadelphia, PA 19103

(215) 977-2266
Fax: (215) 977-2334
rwiener@wolfblock.com

# Music Boxes

Mechanical musical instruments describes any musican instrument that plays by itself: music boxes, band organs, monkey organs, coin pianos, etc. Our specialty is pre-1920, and excludes regular player pianos. Because these instruments vary so widely, and so many different models were made, we will need several good photographs from different angles if we are to accurately appraise what you have.

## DISC MUSIC BOXES:

| | |
|---|---|
| Regina 12" disc music box | $600 |
| Regina 12" disc music box, gum vendor | 2,000 |
| Regina 15-1/2" disc single comb music box | 1,500 |
| Regina 15-1/2" disc double comb music box | 2,000 |
| Regina 20-1/2" disc double comb music box | 3,000 |
| Regina 27" disc double comb music box with folding top | 5,000 |
| Regina 27" disc music box in upright case | 8,000 |
| Regina 15-1/2 disc music box, changes 12 discs automatically | 12,500 |
| Regina 20-1/2" disc music box, changes 12 discs automatically | 12,500 |
| Regina 27" disc music box, changes 12 discs automatically | 13,500 |
| Polyphon 15-1/2 disc double comb music box | 2,000 |
| Polyphon 19-5/8" disc upright music box | 3,500 |
| Polyphon 22-1/4 disc upright music box with bells | 6,500 |
| Polyphon 24-1/2 disc upright music box with base cabinet | 7,000 |
| Symphonion 19-1/8" upright disc music box | 3,000 |
| Symphonion 3-disc upright music box | 15,000 |
| Symphonion 3-disc upright music box with clock | 20,000 |
| Mira 18-1/2 disc music box, table model | 4,000 |
| Mira 18-1/2" disc music box, console floor model | 5,500 |
| Lochmann 24-1/2 disc music box with bells | 9,000 |
| Capital Cuff music box, 4-1/2" cuff | 1,500 |

## CYLINDER MUSIC BOXES:

| | |
|---|---|
| Nicole Freres 13" x 2-1/2" cylinder keywind music box | $800 |
| Nicole Freres 13" x 4" cylinder keywind music box | 3,000 |
| Nicole Freres 17-1/2" x 4" cylinder keywind music box | 6,000 |
| Mermod Freres 14" cylinder music box | 1,000 |
| Mermod Freres 14" cylinder music box with bells | 1,250 |
| Mermod Freres 14" cylinder music box, four cylinders | 2,500 |
| Mermod Freres 20-1/2" cylinder music box, five cylinders, table | 7,500 |
| Mermod Freres 24-1/2" cylinder music box, six cylinders, table | 15,000 |
| Paillard 18" cylinder music box | 1,500 |
| Paillard 18" cylinder music box, four cylinders | 3,500 |
| Paillard 18" cylinder music box, five cylinders, table | 5,000 |
| Snuff box cylinder music box, before 1840 | 250 |
| "Pleriodinique" style music box, multiple cylinders | 10,000 |
| Cylinder music box with six cylinders mounted on "carousel" | 15,000 |

## MECHANICAL BIRDS:

| | |
|---|---|
| Early bird cage, single bird, separate key winds from side | $450 |
| Early bird cage, two birds, separate key winds from side | 750 |
| Early bird cage, three birds, separate key winds from side | 1,000 |
| Twentieth century bird box with singing bird | 300 |
| Early fusee wind bird box with singing bird | 1,000 |
| Automaton with clock and five mechanical birds under glass dome | 2,000 |

## BAND ORGANS:

| | |
|---|---|
| Wurlitzer style 125 band organ, brass trumpets, playing | $12,000 |
| Wurlitzer style 150 band organ, brass trumpets, playing | 16,000 |
| Wurlitzer style 153 band organ, playing | 20,000 |

## ORCHESTRONS:

| | |
|---|---|
| Mills Violano Virtuoso automatic violin, good condition | $8,000 |
| Hupfeld Phonolit, three violins, automatic with piano | 100,000 |
| Seeburg L 44-note cabinet style piano, working | 3,000 |
| Seeburg Eagle style piano with pipes | 5,000 |
| Wurlitzer style H orchestrion, carved female posts | 55,000 |
| Large Weber orchestrion | 15,000 |
| Large Welte orchestrion with "sunburst" metal trumpets | 30,000 |

## MONKEY ORGANS:

| | |
|---|---|
| 25-key Molinari with 38 pipes | $2000 |
| 42-key Bacigalupo with 90 pipes | 5,000 |
| 38-key Frati with 80 pipes and brass trumpets in front | 6,500 |

**Prices Paid by:** Martin Roenigk, Mechantiques
26 Barton Hill                          (203) 267-8682
East Hampton, CT 06424          Fax   (203) 267-1120

# Magic Posters & Memorabilia

I have been actively collecting vintage magic posters and related magicians' memorabilia and ephemera for the past 20 years. It is difficult to put a price on all posters of a particular performer or all posters in a particular category because there may be a great difference in value between a rare poster and a more common one. Therefore, the prices set out below may be close to what I am willing to pay. So contact me and I will make you an offer after I know the specifics about your poster.

Especially with paper items, condition is all important. If something is not properly mounted or is badly torn or folded, stained, etc., it may lower the value of the item. A color photo is always helpful in evaluating an item.

**EXAMPLES OF SPECIFIC MAGICIANS WHOSE POSTERS I BUY.**
**ALL ITEMS ARE FULL COLOR STONE LITHOGRAPHS.**

| | |
|---|---|
| Albini | $500+ |
| Andress | 500+ |
| Bancroft | 500+ |
| Blackstone Sr. | 500+ |
| Brindamour | 500+ |
| Brush | 500+ |
| Carter (Goes litho) | 500+ |
| Chung Ling Soo | 600+ |
| Dante | 400+ |
| T. Nelson Downs | 500+ |
| Germain (Germaine) | 500+ |
| Goldin | 500+ |
| Hardeen | 500+ |
| Herrmann | 850+ |
| Houdini | 1000+ |
| Kellar | 750+ |
| Servais Leroy | 500+ |
| Maro | 350+ |
| Nicola | 500+ |
| Powell | 500+ |
| Raymond | 500+ |
| Rameses | 500+ |
| Rouclere | 500+ |
| Thurston (Otis) | 350+ |
| Thurston (Strobridge) | 600+ |
| Valadon | 500+ |
| Von Arx | 400+ |
| Wood | 500+ |

*Price Paid $1000+ each*

This is not intended to be a complete list. If you have a poster of a magician not named on this list, call or write anyway... I also collect stock posters issued by litho companies. These may not always have the name of a specific performer but are still of some interest to me.

I am not interested in posters depicting Carter (Otis litho), George, Heaney, Irving, Fak Hong or Kar-Mi unless your price is very low. I am not interested in reproductions of posters or contemporary magic posters such as David Copperfield.

### OTHER MAGIC EPHEMERA & MEMORABILIA

**Childrens' magic sets**, including Mysto, Aladdin, Spear. Expecially interested in English, French & German sets, worth $25-250, depending on rarity, condition, etc. Sets that are mostly plastic from the 1950's or later are usually of little interest.

**Houdini collectibles** – signed or unsigned photos, letters and postcards, scrapbooks, paper advertising, clippings, handcuffs, books and pamphlets will bring from $35 to $500 or more, depending on the item, rarity and condition. Not interested in *Big Little Books*.

**Programs, broadsides and other magic magicians' advertising:** Worth from 50¢ to $500 or more, depending on the item, its condition and rarity.

**Give-aways from magician's** postcards, signed photos, pinbacks, tokens, throw-out cards, pamphlets, door-hangers, sheet music, handbills, etc., will bring you from $3 to $300, depending on item, rarity and condition.

**Product advertising** and character items with a magic theme: For example, Mickey Mouse Magician tin toy, magician bank.

**Prints & Engravings** with magic themes (such as the cups and balls trick): Worth $5-500, depending on rarity and condition.

**Magic apparatus** manufactured before 1950: Prices depend on condition and scarcity. It is helpful if instructions are included. Good condition only. Home-made apparatus is usually of little value. Also, I am not looking for jokes or puzzles.

**Hard-cover books:** From $1 to $1,000 paid, depending on the book.

**Soft cover magic books:** pre-1900 only, worth $10-1,000, depending on the book, its condition and scarcity.

**Magic magazines:** Only interested in complete runs of early (pre-1920) magazines. $50-500 for the run, depending on the magazine. Not interested in *Genii, Linking Ring MUM* or *Tops.*

**Magic catalogs:** Only pre-1925 catalogs in good shape $25-250, depending on the catalog, its condition & rarity.

Price paid: $1000+

Price paid; $600+

| Prices Paid by: | Ken Trombly | (202) 887-5000 days |
|---|---|---|
| | 7112 Lock Lomond Drive | Fax: (202) 457-0342 |
| | Bethesda, MD 20817 | (301) 320-2360 eves |
| | To sell posters only: (800) 673-8158 | trombly@erols.com |
| | **Please don't send anything on approval. Call or write first.** | |

# Vintage TVs and Radios

- **1920s mechanical TVs** (spinning disc with neon tube). These were made by Baird, Western, Jenkins, Empire, ICA, SeeAll, Daven, etc. **$750-5,000**
- **1930s B&W TVs** (no channel 7 through 13). With 5", 9" or 12" picture tube, in a kit, table top, console or mirror-in-lid cabinet. RCA TRK and TT5, GE with pushbutton tuner, DuMont 180, Andrea, Don Lee, etc. **1,000-5,000**
- **1939-1952 color TVs** by CBS, GE, Smith & Klein, Zenith, RCA. With up to 3 tubes (5"-16" diameter), color wheel or color drum. **1,000-5,000**
- **1945 to 1975 TVs**: very small or very unusual sets. **up to 250**
- **1920-1930s** crystal and tube radios, factory or home-made. **up to 500**
- **1930-1940** Deco radios with colored Catalin or colored celluloid, chrome, plexiglass, or mirrored cases, by Air King, FADA, Sparton, RCA, Emerson, Motorola, Kadette, etc. **250-10,000**

- Novelty tube-type radios such as Emerson Mickey Mouse or Snow White, World's Fair, Rudolph, Bozo, world globe, bowling ball, baseball, etc. **up to 1,000**
- **Transistor radios:** USA-made or Japanese. **Send list.**
- **Tubes:** new, used, boxed, or loose. **Wanted. Send list.**
- **Microphones**, signs, displays, advertising. **Wanted!**

*1939 RCA TT5*
*Paying $2,000*

# Cameras and View Master

- **Nikon and Canon** cameras, lenses, motor drives, etc **$200-5,000**
- **Leica** cameras, Leitz lenses and accessories, old or new **up to 1,500**
- **Kodak:** Super 620, World's Fair, other unusual cameras **up to 1,000**
- **Polaroids:** only model #180, 190, 195 (no other Polaroids!) **100**
- **Movie:** 16mm and 35mm cameras **up to 250**
- **Press and View**: Graflex, Linhoff, etc. **Wanted**. (**Stereo cameras** have 2 lenses, side-by-side, which make a double slide. 3D viewers and 3D projectors have two lenses and show a stereoscopic image.)

*Stereo Wollensak*
*Paying $500*

- **Stereo cameras:** Stereo Realist, Revere, Wollensak, Linex, Belplasca, Rolleidoscop, Verascope F40, Windsor, TDC, etc. **75-750**
- **Stereo MACRO** cameras: Stereo Realist "Macro" complete outfit and Donaldson bellows-type stereo Macro camera, complete **2,500**
- **Stereo viewers:** Realist, Airequipt, Kodaslide, etc. **up to 125**
- **Stereo projectors:** TDC, B&H, Realist, Compco, Triad, etc. **up to 450**
- **View Master** "Personal" camera with case and film cutter. **up to 250**
- **View Master** Stereomatic 500 (two-lens) projector with case. **150**
- **View Master** Model "D" focusing viewer. **50**
- **View Master reels** and Tru-Vue rolls. **Wanted! Please send list.**

**\*\* We buy complete Radio/TV shops and Camera and Photo shops! \*\***
*We offer a free evaluation of your old radios, televisions and cameras: just send a photo of your items, and include a SASE*

| Prices Paid by: | Harry Poster | 24 hour phone (201) 794-9606 |
| --- | --- | --- |
| | P.O. Box 1883-SP | Fax (201) 794-9553 |
| | South Hackensack, NJ 07606 | hposter@worldnet.att.net |

# Radios

The development of the radio industry was rapid during the years 1921 to 1940. Radios went through many physical changes and circuit designs in this short period, which makes it of interest to most collectors of radios. In the early 1920's radios were mainly of the battery operated type, usually contained in a wooden case with a lift-top lid. After 1928 almost all radios were plugged into an AC wall outlet. People familiar with radios can use cabinet styles to date most radios.

## RADIOS WANTED:

| | |
|---|---|
| 1921 to 1927 battery operated radios – models with 1 to 3 tubes | $30-300 |
| 1921 to 1927 battery operated radios – models with 4 to 8 tubes | 40-175 |
| 1920's crystal radios (use no tubes), must be factory made! | 25-200 |
| 1928 to 1930 AC operated table models, wood cabinets only | 25-75 |
| 1928 to 1930 AC operated table models, metal cabinets | 10-35 |
| 1930 to 1934 cathedral shaped radios (rounded tops) | 50-200 |
| 1930 to 1938 tombstone shaped radios (tall w/flat top) | 35-100 |
| 1930's floor models (I don't usually buy these unless exceptional) | 25-150 |
| 1930's table or mantle sets (small radios less than 12" wide) | 10-50 |

Radios of Bakelite or plastic are not wanted unless of unusual design or color.

## RADIO SPEAKERS:

| | |
|---|---|
| Horn type used with 1920's radios | $25-95 |
| 1920's cone speakers (round, open framed paper front type) | 20-75 |
| 1930's speakers enclosed in wood or metal cabinets | 10-25 |

## RADIO LITERATURE:

| | |
|---|---|
| Riders Service manuals, Volumes 1-23, each | $7-20 |
| 1920/30's radio catalogs for companies such as Barawik, Allied, Lafayette | 5-20 |
| 1920' radio magazines: Radio News, Popular Radio, Radio Broadcast | 3-10 |
| 1930's radio magazines: Radio Craft, Short-Wave Craft, others | 2-5 |

Note: during the 1920/30's there were over 40 titles of magazines

## RADIO TUBES & PARTS:

I'll buy most early 4-prong radio tubes, either new or used, and most other tubes up to 1940 if new. Because there are thousands of different types made it is impossible to give an accurate range of prices. Also buy all types of radio parts for the servicing and repair of radios such as transformers, dials, knobs, and other new old-stock parts.

As items wanted are of a very technical nature it is very helpful it complete description of items is given. Sketches or photos of radios are helpful. Will pay for all photos or other costs you incur to send complete information.

**Also buy early tipped light bulbs, telegraph items, old phones, radio advertising signs and ephemera.**

---

| | | |
|---|---|---|
| **Prices Paid by:** | Gary Schneider | |
| | 14310 Ordner Drive | Days (216) 251-3714 |
| | Cleveland, Ohio 44136 | After 9 PM (216) 582-3094 |

---

# 78 rpm Phonograph Records

Most everyone has a stack of old 78's somewhere - in the closet, basement, barn or attic. However, only a very small percentage have significant value, and condition is as important in this field as in any other. Rare records are often encountered, however. So records are definitely worth checking out before they are given away. The following information will give you a general idea of what to look for.

*(All prices quoted are for records in excellent condition.)*

### JAZZ, BLUES, CAJUN AND COUNTRY RECORDS FROM 1925-1935

There are literally thousands of artists and labels in this category that are of significant value. The following label series each contain records that could be valued at $20, $50, even $100 or more!

Brunswick (lightning bolt label) 100-500 and 7000 series
Bluebird (buff-colored label) 2000 and 5000 series
Champion 15-16,000 series
Columbia 14-15,000 series
Gennett 5-7,000 series
Okeh 8,000; 40-41,000 and 45,000 series
Paramount 3,000 and 12-13,000 series
Perfect 0100-0200 series
Victor 23,000; V-38,000; and V-40,000 series
Vocalion 1-5000 and 14-15,000 series

*Operatic G & T    $100*

Please note that not every record that falls within these number ranges has collector value, but a great many do. Further, there are many more jazz, blues, Cajun and country records that are very valuable which are not found in this list!

### EARLY CLASSICAL AND OPERATIC RECORDS MADE PRIOR TO 1910

| | |
|---|---|
| Red label Victor "Monarch" or "Deluxe" records | $20-100 |
| One-sided Columbia "Grand Opera" disc records | 150-500 |
| Fonotipia or Odeon records | 10-500 |
| Gramophone & Typewriter label records | 15-1,000 |
| Operatic Zonophone records | 20-1,500 |

Please note that later classical records and album sets are generally of lesser value and are therefore usually of little interest.

### PICTURE RECORDS

| | |
|---|---|
| RCA Victor | $150-2,000 |
| Vogue | 20-2,500 |
| 7" Children's Picture Record | 5-25 |
| Mercury | 150 |
| Talk-O-Photo | 200 |
| Other Picture Discs | 5-500 |

Generally speaking, we want any 78 rpm picture record you have, regardless of scarcity, value or condition.

*RCA picture disk    $400*

Race Series Vocalion  $250

| | |
|---|---|
| Herwin | Flexo |
| Herschel | Sunrise |
| Black Patti | Superior |
| Electra | Polk |
| Electradisk | Merritt |
| QRS | Buddy |
| Vitaphone | Nation's Forum |
| Black Swan | Wonder |
| Kalamazoo | Blu-Disc |
| KKK | Berliner |
| Autograph | Sunshine |
| Gem | Harmograph |
| Timely Tunes | Rialto |
| Hollywood | Sun |
| Vulcan | Phonolamp |
| Nordskog | Chautauqua |

## ODD AND UNUSUAL LABELS

This is only a partial list! I will pay $10-300 for examples of these and many other labels if they are in excellent condition.

## EARLY ROCK AND ROLL FROM THE 1950'S

Look for labels like Sun, Imperial, Checker, Jubilee, Specialty, etc., and for artists like Buddy Holly, Elvis Presley, Chuck Berry and Little Richard. Prices paid will range from $3-250, but records must be in excellent condition with very little or no wear!

## CYLINDER RECORDS

| | |
|---|---|
| Brown wax cylinders | $5-100 |
| Pink, purple, white or orange celluloid cylinders | 50-200 |
| Any cylinders measuring 6" in length or 5" in diameter | 50-100 |
| Any blue cylinders numbered between 5000 and 5750 | 5-50 |
| Any cylinders with operatic or historical content | 5-100 |

Do not attempt to clean your cylinders. Avoid touching the surface of the cylinder with your fingers, as this could cause major problems as well. DO NOT attempt to play your cylinders, as they can easily be ruined by improper equipment!

### Important!

**We do not buy** the following: big band, Hawaiian, sacred, popular and traditional songs, popular instrumental selections or album sets. We also do not buy 45rpm or 33rpm long play records!

### We are also interested in purchasing wind-up phonographs and antique music boxes!

| **Prices Paid by:** | Nauck's Vintage Records |
|---|---|
| | 6323 Inway Drive |
| | Spring, TX 77389 |
| | (281) 370-7899    Fax  (281) 251-7023    nauck@78rpm.com |

To obtain our illustrated wants list with additional categories included, please send $2.00 plus a long SASE. This brochure includes instructions for listing, packing and shipping your records. If the size and value of your collection warrants, we will be happy to travel to your location for an on-site evaluation!

# 78 rpm Phonograph Records

Valuable 78's are usually obscure and unfamiliar to non-collectors. Because the field is so diverse, if you describe your records to me and include an SASE, upon request I will send you fliers with information appropriate to the kind of records you have.

Subjects of these "free" mailers include: SCARCE & UNUSUAL LABELS (with prices paid); LABELS/ARTISTS of the 1940s/1950s (many **rock 'n' roll** 78s are saleable); SALEABLE RECORDS by "POP" and COUNTRY STARS whose records are mostly common. My **PERSONAL WANT LIST** of l920s jazz, dance band, etc., specifies records for which I'll pay premium prices, such as these few examples: $100 each for **Vocalion** 15703, 15705, 15712, 15740, 15750, 15761, 15763, 15768, 15769, 15779, 15784, 15792, I5797, 15805, 15810, 15834; and $50 each for **Vocalion** 15665, 15666, 15724, 15728, 15815, 15819, 15828, 15836, 15837 (for the first acceptable copy of each sent me, as provided in my send-outs).

**YOUR LISTS of records are always welcome**. Required information: label, record number, artist/band, and song titles. **Time-saving tip:** organize all records by label, then numerically within each label, before making list. It will save us both a lot of time and work!   Include a S.A.S.E.

### "SHELLAC SHACK'S WANT LIST OF 78 RPM RECORDS"

For the information and convenience of sellers, I offer my copyrighted, 72-page booklet, which contains buying prices for thousands of 78 RPM records on commonly found labels such as Bluebird, Brunswick, Columbia, Decca, and Victor, listed by record number with the specific price I pay for each disc. This is a detailed, "live" buying offer, backed by cash, not a vague reference. Included are pictures of many labels, packing and shipping information.  This booklet is sent for only $2.00 which is refunded when records are sold to me.  It is not necessary, however, to buy the booklet or anything else from me in order to offer/sell me records.

---

**"American Premium Record Guide"** by L.R. Docks, published by Books Americana, will provide those interested with a more comprehensive view of popular record collecting. It lists 78s, 45s, and LPs, 1900-1965, including jazz, blues, dance bands, hillbilly, rock 'n' roll, rhythm & blues, rockabilly, celebrity recordings, etc. Included are photographs of 1600 labels, a bibliography and list of publications. Check your bookstore, or write to me for more information.

---

**Prices Paid by:**   L.R. "Les" Docks
P.O. Box 691035
San Antonio, Texas  78269
Fax  (210) 492-6489

# Musical Instruments

I pay cash for guitars by Gibson, Gretsch, Fender, Martin, Rickenbacker, Epiphone, Stromberg, D'Angelico, D'Aquisto, Guild, Vox, National, Dobro, Maurer, Prairie State, etc. Interested in all used vintage American instruments, banjos, mandolins, ukuleles and amps. Prices are guidelines for clean, original instruments. Modifications lower value much as 50%.

## FENDER GUITARS

Fender guitars were made in Fullerton, California as were amplifiers and other musical instruments. All US-made Fender instruments are of interest and have some value. Among them, these are the most significant. Dates of manufacture are determined by serial numbers and markings.

### Fender Stratocaster Guitars

| | |
|---|---|
| 1950's maple fingerboard, sunburst finish | $3,000-6,000 |
| 1960's rosewood fingerboard, sunburst finish | 2,500 |
| 1960's rosewood fingerboard, solid color | 3,500 up |
| 1970's large headstock, three bolt neck | 650-1,200 |

More if hardware is gold plated.

### Fender Telecaster or Esquire Guitars

| | |
|---|---|
| 1950's Broadcaster, see thru butterscotch | $5,000-10,000 |
| 1950's maple fingerboard, lemon finish, orig. | 2,500-5,000 |
| 1960's rosewood fingerboard, lemon finish | 1,500-2,500 |
| 1960's rosewood fingerboard, solid color | 2,500-4,000 |
| 1960's sunburst with white binding on body | 2,000-3,000 |
| 1960's paisley floral finish on body | 1,800-2,500 |

More if hardware is gold plated.

### Fender Jaguar & Jazzmaster Guitars

| | |
|---|---|
| 1960's sunburst finish, all original | $600-up |
| 1960's solid colors (blue, red, gold, white, etc.) | 800-up |

More if hardware is gold plated.

### Fender Lap Steel Guitars (electric Hawaiian guitars)

| | |
|---|---|
| 1950's six or eight strings, any finish | $100-450 |

### Fender Basses

| | |
|---|---|
| 1960's Jazz Bass, sunburst finish | $600-1,800 |
| 1950's Precision Bass, sunburst finish | 900-2,500 |
| 1960's Precision Bass, sunburst finish | 500-1,000 |

## GRETSCH GUITARS

Most Gretsch guitars are worth at least $500. Some of the finer models listed below, if original, are worth considerably more. Prices are for unmodified examples with original cases. Value is higher is original advertising is included (catalog, price tag, invoice, photos, strap, etc.) and lower if modified.

| | |
|---|---|
| 50's White Penguin, white solid body | $10,000 up |
| 50's White Falcon, single cutaway | 3,500-8,000 |
| 60's White Falcon, double cutaway | 1,500-3,000 |
| 50's Country Gentleman, single cutaway | 2,000-2,500 |
| 50's Chet Atkins 6120, orange,single cutaway | 2,000-3,500 |
| 50's Roundup, orange, "B" brand, solid body | 1,400-2,500 |
| 50's-60's Duo Jet solid body, red, sparkle | 1,000-2,500 |
| Synchromatic models, non-electric | 500-2,500 |
| Gretsch amplifiers, with western motif | 400-800 |
| Gretsch advertising, clocks, signs, catalogs | 100-500 |

## GIBSON Les Paul Model Guitars

Most Gibson guitars are valued above $200. Some models are very valuable if all original and unmodified. Additionally, old instruments in poor condition have value for parts with some 1950's parts alone worth over $500! Naturally, an appraisal is worthwhile.

| | |
|---|---|
| 50's-60's sunburst Les Paul standard | $15,000 up |
| 50's gold top, white pickups (P-90's) | 3,000-10,000 |
| 50's gold top, metal pickups (Humbuckers) | 10,000 up |
| 60's gold top, white pickups (P-90's) | 800-1,800 |
| 50's Les Paul Junior, sunburst or red finish | 950-1,500 |
| 50's Les Paul TV model, yellow finish | 1,200-2,000 |
| 70's Les Paul deluxe, custom, standard | 600 up |
| 80's Les Paul custom, standard | 600 up |

## GIBSON GUITARS

| | |
|---|---|
| 20's L-5 archtop, Loar signature, dot inlays | $5,000-up |
| 30's-50's L-5 archtop guitar, no pickups | 2,000-up |
| 30's EB-150 "Charlie Christian" model, pickup | 2,000-up |
| 30's-40's Super 400 guitar, no pickups | 5,000-up |
| 60's Super 400 CES, L-5CES, with pickups | 4,000-up |
| 59 ES-335TDN, natural finish, dot inlay | $3,500-8,000 |
| 59 ES-345TDN, natural finish | 3,000-6,000 |
| 58-62 ES-335, dot inlay, stop TPC, sunburst | 2,000-5,000 |
| 62-69 ES-335, orange label | 950-2,000 |
| 50's Flying V guitar, solid body, "V" shaped | 30,000 up |
| 50's Explorer guitar, solid body, "Z" shaped | 30,000 up |
| 30's J-200 guitar, flat top, rosewood body | 10,000 up |
| 30's Jumbo guitar, flat top, rosewood body | 5,000 up |

## MARTIN GUITARS

All Martin guitars are valuable. Prices range from $500 for the all mahogany 0-15 model to $50,000 for the pre-WWII D-45 model with abalone borders. Martin ukes are worth at least $150-900 for most models. Martin mandolins are worth far less unless ornamented. Prices below are for the most desireable models which I'm always interested in buying.

| | |
|---|---|
| 30's-40's 000-45, pearl trim, rosewood | $20,000 up |
| 60's D-45, pearl trim, rosewood back | 10,000 up |
| 30's D-28, rosewood back and sides | 10,000 up |
| 40's D-28, rosewood back and sides | 7,500 up |
| 50's D-28, rosewood back and sides | 2,000-3,500 |
| 30's OM-28, rosewood back and sides | 5,000-9,500 |
| 30's OM-45, pearl trim, rosewood | 25,000 up |
| 39-42 D-45, pearl trim, rosewood | 50,000 up |
| 20's-30's Hawaiian models | 500-2,500 |

KOAWOOD MODELS, TENORS, ARCHTOPS, FLAT TOPS, ALL MODELS BOUGHT

## OTHER MAKERS

| | |
|---|---|
| 30's-50's D'Angelico guitars, any original | $20,000 up |
| 30's-50's Stromberg guitars, any original | 7,500-25,000 |
| 60's Rickenbacker guitars, 6 or 12 strong | 500-1,800 |
| 30's National metal guitars, ukes, mandolins | 500-5,000 |

## AMPLIFIERS

| | |
|---|---|
| 50's Fender Bassman, tweed, 4-10" speakers | $800-1,200 |
| 50's Fender Super, tweed coveirng | 550-1,000 |
| 60's Vox AC30 w/ top boost, combo with stand | 500-1,000 |
| 50's Fender tweed amps, all models | 250 up |
| 60's Fender Vobrolux reverb, deluxe, super | 300 up |
| 60's Marshall amplifiers, half-stacks, stacks | 900-1,500 |
| 30's-60's Gibson amplifiers, all original | 150-1,000 |

## BANJOS

| | |
|---|---|
| 20's-30's Gibson Mastertone banjos | $900-6,500 |
| 20's-30's Bacon and Day Silverbell banjos | 700-7,500 |
| 20's-30's Paramount banjos | 450-4,500 |
| 20's-30's Vega banjos | 150-4,500 |
| 1900's Fairbanks banjos, Whyte Laydie, etc. | 350-9,000 |
| 1900's S.S. Stewart banjos, fancy inlays | 500-5,000 |
| 20's Ludwig banjos, banjo-ukes | 250-2,500 |

Please note: I am a serious buyer and do not trifle with serious sellers. I pay cash for good instruments, accurately and honestly described. If you have or know of an instrument for sale, please call with a full description including serial number and asking price. Serious finders are encouraged to contact me. If I buy the instrument, I will pay all shipping costs plus reimburse you for your phone call to me!

---

**Prices Paid by:** Steve Senerchia, The Music Man
300 Quaker Lane, Suite #7
Warwick, RI 02886
musicman@tiac.net

(401) 821-2865
Fax (401) 823-4728
www.tiac.net/users/musicman

---

# Movie Posters

I will pay the following prices for American One-Sheets (27" x 41") in excellent condition:

| | |
|---|---:|
| American Graffiti - 40x60 or larger | $60 |
| Angels With Dirty Faces | 3,000 |
| Animal House - 40x60 or larger | 60 |
| Animal Crackers | 4,000 |
| Baby Takes a Bow | 2,000 |
| Black Cat (1934) - 1-sheet | 25,000 |
| Black Pirate (Fairbanks) | 5,000 |
| Blue Angel - 1-sheet or Larger | 10,000 |
| Bordertown | 5,000 |
| Breakfast at Tiffany's - 1-sheet | 500 |
| Bride of Frankenstein - 1-sheet | 60,000 |
| Bringing Up Baby | 2,500 |
| Broken Arrow - 1-sheet | 75 |
| Cabaret - 3-sheet or larger | 60 |
| Captain Blood | 3,000 |
| Casablanca | 3,000 |
| Citizen Kane | 9,000 |
| Cleopatra (1934) Full-Colbert 3-sheet | 2,500 |
| Creature from Black Lagoon, 1sheet or larger | 2,000 |
| Crime School | 2,000 |
| Dangerous | 4,000 |
| Day the Earth Stood Still 1 sheet or lrgr | 2,500 |
| Dinner at 8 - 1-sheet | 5,000 |
| Dr. Jekyll & Mr. Hyde (Barrymore, 1920) | 24,000 |
| Dr. Jekyll & Mr. Hyde (1932) 1-sheet or larger | 18,000 |
| Dracula insert | 20,000 |
| Dracula | 100,000 |
| Enter the Dragon - 40x60 or larger | 60 |
| Flying Down to Rio - 1-sheet | 10,000 |
| Footlight Parade | 8,500 |
| Frankenstein (style A or B) | 100,000 |
| General, The | 12,000 |

| | |
|---|---:|
| Girl From 10th Avenue | 6,000 |
| Gold Rush | 15,000 |
| Gold Diggers of 1935 | 3,000 |
| Gone With The Wind | 5,000 |
| Gone with the Wind - 40x60 or 3-sheet | 6,500 |
| Graduate - 1-sheet or larger | 50 |
| Hallelujah! | 9,000 |
| Hound of the Baskervilles (1939) 1-sheet or 3-sheet | 6,000 |
| Hunchback of Notre Dame (Chaney) | 16,000 |
| Invisible Ray - 1-sheet | 16,000 |
| Invisible Man - 1-sheet or 3-sheet | 25,000 |
| It's a Wonderful Life-1-sheet or larger | 3,000 |
| Jesse James - 1-sheet or larger | 2,000 |
| Jezebel - 1-sheet or 3-sheet | 6,000 |
| King Kong (1933) - 1-sheet or larger | 55,000 |
| King Kong Press Book | 1,800 |
| Little Caesar | 13,000 |
| London After Midnight | 20,000 |
| London After Midnight title card | 4,000 |
| Lost World | 20,000 |
| Maltese Falcon | 3,000 |
| Man From Planet X | 2,000 |
| Mark of Zorro (1940) 1-sheet or larger | 3,000 |
| Mata Hari | 4,500 |
| Metropolis (American release) | 60,000 |
| Mummy, The insert | 20,000 |
| Mummy, The (style C or D) | 70,000 |
| Mummy, The 1/2 sheet | 20,000 |
| Old Dark House | 17,000 |
| Out of the Past (1947) 1-sheet or lrgr | 1,000 |
| Petrified Forest - 1-sheet or larger | 5,000 |
| Public Enemy - 1-sheet | 12,000 |
| Puttin' On The Ritz | 3,000 |
| Raven (1935) - 1-sheet | 25,000 |
| Razor's Edge (1946) Norman Rockwell 1-sheet or 3-sheet | 1500 |
| Rebecca | 1,800 |
| Rocky Horror Picture Show | 50 |
| Roman Holiday - 1-sheet | 100 |
| Sabrina - 1-sheet | 100 |
| Scarlet Empress (artwork) 22x28 or lrgr | 5,000 |
| Shane - 1-sheet (near mint) | 500 |
| Son of Frankenstein | 5,500 |
| Son of Kong | 13,000 |
| Steamboat Willie | 60,000 |
| Superman (1941 Fleischer) | 5,000 |
| Superman & the Mole Men | 1,000 |
| Tale of Two Cities (1935) - 1-sheet | 3,000 |
| The 39 Steps | 3,000 |
| Thin Man - 22x28 or larger | 2,500 |
| This Gun For Hire | 1,500 |
| War of the Worlds 1/2 sheet w/saucers | 2,000 |
| War of the Worlds - British Quad | 2,000 |
| Werewolf of London | 17,000 |
| Winchester '73 - Insert/22x28/1-sheet | 100 |
| Wizard of Oz | 4,000 |
| Wolfman | 5,500 |

**Prices Paid by:** Dwight Cleveland
P.O. Box 10922
Chicago, IL 60610

# Golf

## Golf Clubs, Memorabilia & Golfing Antiques

Collector of good original quality equipment. Prefer items that have not been restored, refinished, cleaned or repaired.

Common wood shaft clubs from 1915-1937 were manufactured in the millions. Of these, 70-85% of them have value of $5-50 in general. Most have no collector interest other than being wall hangers. Some of these makers are Wilson, Spalding, Macgregor, Burke, H&B. Common clubs have marks such as dot punched faces, dot-dash faces, caps at grip end of shafts, heads marked with yardage, head marked match set, chrome plated heads.

### Common Wood Shafts, 1915-1937

| | |
|---|---|
| Woods | $5-50 |
| Irons | 5-20 |
| Putters | 10-75 |
| Smooth face clubs (irons) | 115-120 |
| Spalding spring face | 250-1,200 |
| Spalding cran iron (wood insert on face) | 200-1,200 |
| Spalding Seely patent irons | 300-1,000 |
| Hagen concave face sand club | 150-450 |
| Spalding, Macgregor, Wright & Ditson, Burke, Forgan and many other splice neck woods | 75-500+ |

### Spliced Woods

| | |
|---|---|
| by makers McEwan, Park, Simpson, The Spalding, Morris, Dunn, Scott, etc. | $220-1,200 |

### Long Nose Play Clubs

| | |
|---|---|
| Mid-1800 thru 1890's – Allan, Philp, Anderson, Ayres, Dunn, Forgan, Gibson, Park, Patrick, etc. | $200-2100+ |

### Classic Clubs 1940-1970's

| | |
|---|---|
| Drivers | $50-150 |
| Wood sets | 150-500 |
| Iron sets | 75-500 |

Seeking top quality playable classic.

### Macgregor Woods

| | |
|---|---|
| M85, M75, TPT, WW Penna, SS1, 693, Armour Promodel, Hogan Promodel, George Bayer models | $75-500+ |
| Tommy Armour putters marked silver scot ironmaster with codes as 3852, IM, IMG, IMG5, IMG6, etc. | 40-450 |

### Putters

| | |
|---|---|
| Ping Putter, Scottsdale models B66, 67, 69, 1A, 11A, 111A, etc. | $50-250 |
| Wilson - 8802, 8813, Arnold Palmer, etc. | 250-800 |

### Irons

| | |
|---|---|
| Ping Ballmatic, model 69, K1, K11, K111, Ping Eye, Ping Eye 2, Ping Eye II Plus sets | $200-500+ |

### Gold Balls

| | |
|---|---|
| Feather balls | $300-1,500+ |
| Gutta percha balls | 30-600 |
| Rubber core balls 1895-1930 | 5-100 |
| Mesh pattern balls | 5-50 |
| Post 1935 modern balls | 5-30 |

### Golf Books

Interested in 1st printings, dated. Prior to 1940

| | |
|---|---|
| Books up to 1920 | $10-400+ |
| Books 1920-1930 | 5-50 |
| Books 1930-1970 | 5-40 |
| Manufacturers equipment catalogues 1895-1945 | 10-65 |

### China & Pottery

Many companies produced plates, jugs, multi-handled mugs, bowls, vases, humidors, beakers, match stick holders, etc.

Made by Carltonware, Copeland Spode, Doulton, Gerz, Grimwades Ltd., Lenox, Minton, O'Hara Dial Co., Sleepyeye, Wedgewood, Weller, etc.

| | |
|---|---|
| Prices paid vary greatly depending on manufacturer, type of piece, colors used, and subject | $50-5,000 |

### General Golf

The different golf items of interest to me are just too numerous to list. Here are a few.

Contestant badges, trophies of famous players and courses, tournament programs, autographs, early photos, tintypes, postal stamps, 1st day issues, prints, printings, pocket watches, match safes, ink stands, flasks, bookends, door stops, bronze statuary, cigarette cards, post cards of early golfers and courses. Golf games, slot machines, pinball machines, early golf films, instructional albums, etc.

Any item no matter how rare is only worth what a buyer is willing to pay. Photo copies, photographs and complete description of items offered for sale are very helpful. Sometimes item must be in hand to determine the fairest and most accurate price I can pay you.

**Also seeking early tennis and boxing related equipment and memorabilia.**

---

**Prices Paid by:** Richard Regan
293 Winter Street, #5
Hanover, MA 02339

(617) 826-3537
foregolf@tiac.net

---

# Sports

Curator of the Monterey Bay Sports Museum is buying memorabilia

**We are always looking to increase our displays, and I'll pay the following prices in order to enhance the museum:**

Any and all 19th century advertising/display
posters that depict sports figures, sports
card sets, testimonials for products
of the time      $1,000-100,000
An original set/pair of 19th cen.
fingerless baseball **gloves**      1,000-1500
19th cen. baseball **bats**      200 up
Pre-1940 felt **pennants** from football,
baseball and boxing matches      50-1,000 ea.
19th century football **uniform**      1000
Especially interested in larger
display items, such as large
banners and display pieces      500 up
Tickets: full tickets and stubs
   1910 Johnson/Jeffries fight      500/100
   Corbett vs. Sullivan      750/275
   1919 World Series      2,000/650
   1932 World Series      800/400
   Rose Bowl tickets; all years      100-1,000
   Any and all sports tickets from pre-1970

$ $ $ PAID $ $ $

**Early Sports Bronzes & Statues**

$500 and up

**Original fight posters**
John vs. Jeffries 1910      $1,000
J.L. Sullivan vs. Corbett      3,000
Dempsey vs. Tunney 1927      600
Any Rocky Marciano      200 up

**Film posters advertising prize fights**
and/or other sports. We will pay a
good price depending on the event      $100 up
**Sheet music that has a sports theme**
Here are some examples:
Ty Cobb "King of Clubs"      $400
Oh You Jeffries      125
19th cen. baseball sheet music      100-1,000 ea.

*Boxing posters wanted. Will pay $500 for this one.*

Circa 1930's
football poster.
I'll pay $500 for it!

Circa 1888
baseball cabinet
photo. Will pay
$750 for these.

We will pay a premium price for a goodly number of sports related articles that will help us create a bigger and better museum. Try us for friendly service and competitive buying prices. Your pieces, treasured or simply brokered, will arrive at a location where they can be enjoyed by many people of all ages and backgrounds.

We can also arrange a caption for any pieces we buy from an individual, so your name can be attributed to the item in the museum.

Thanks for considering us.

**Prices Paid by:** John Buonaguidi
Monterey Bay Sports Museum
883 Lighthouse Avenue
Monterey, CA 93940
Days: (831) 655-2363   Eves: (831) 375-7345   sportmsm@redshift.com

# Baseball & Sports Memorabilia

Collecting sports memorabilia has become very popular in recent years. Old autographs, programs, team yearbooks, ticket stubs to famous or championship games or matches, pins picturing athletes and advertising posters picturing athletes are highly desirable. However, remember condition is critical. Please, feel free, to contact me if you have any sports memorabilia to sell.

## Autographs

| | |
|---|---|
| Babe Ruth | $300-2,000 |
| Lou Gehrig | 500-3,000 |
| Roy Campanella | 100-350 |
| Roger Maris | 50-200 |
| Tris Speaker | 100-1,500 |
| Walter Johnson | 150-1500 |
| Bobby Jones (golfer) | 200-700 |
| Jack Johnson (boxer) | 200-650 |
| Ty Cobb | 150-1,500 |
| Jackie Robinson | 100-350 |
| Joe Dimaggio | 20-100 |
| Thurman Munson | 75-400 |
| Christy Mathewson | 500-3,000 |
| Roberto Clemente | 75-700 |
| Joe Louis (boxer) | 50-200 |
| Vince Lombardi (football) | 75-200 |

I am also buying autographs of any deceased, well know athlete. Please do not offer me autographs of living athletes except for Joe Dimaggio.

## Team Yearbooks

| | |
|---|---|
| 1950 NY Yankees (called a Sketch Book) | $50-125 |
| 1950's NY Yankees Yearbooks (official version only) | 50-100 |
| 1955 Brooklyn Dodgers Yearbooks | 50-125 |
| 1950's Brooklyn Dodgers Yearbooks | 40-75 |
| 1941 Brooklyn Dodgers Yearbook | 50-100 |
| 1942 Brooklyn Dodgers Yearbook | 100-250 |
| 1962 NY Mets Yearbook | 75-150 |

I am also buying other team yearbooks from the 1950's and earlier.

## Programs

| | |
|---|---|
| 1903 World Series Program | $10,000 +up |
| 1927 World Series Program | 200-700 |
| 1955 World Series Program | 40-75 |
| 1969 World Series Program | 40-75 |
| Super Bowl I Program | 75-150 |

I am also buying other World Series programs before 1957 and most Super Bowl programs and championship boxing.

## Ticket Stubs

| | |
|---|---|
| 1903 World Series | $1,000-2,000 |
| 1927 World Series | 100-250 |
| 1955 World Series | 25-50 |

I am also buying ticket stubs to World Series games before 1979, and stubs to any boxing and football championships. I will pay much higher prices for full unused tickets to these events.

## Pins and Advertising Posters

Anything picturing Mickey Mantle, Babe Ruth, Joe Dimaggio, Roger Maris, Lou Gehrig, Ty Cobb, Joe Louis and any other well known athlete is wanted by me. Contact me if you have any of those items for sale.

Walter Johnson $450 if autograph

Ticket stub 1923 World Series $150

Ty Cobb autograph    pay $150

Roger Maris autograph    pay $50

Jackie Robinson autograph    pay $100

Cy Young autograph    pay $150

# Fishing Tackle

## FISHING LURES, REELS & RELATED ITEMS

I'm always buying fishing tackle items pre-1940. I'm a private collector, not a dealer, so I'll pay retail prices for items to go into my collection. I buy single items or complete collections. I use UPS and we can complete our deal within 72 hours, start to finish.

**LURES** Good condition means I pay more. Some company names are Heddon, Shakespeare, Creek Chub Bait Co., South Bend, Pflueger. Look for glass eyes, multi-colored paint, lots of hooks, spinners and attachments, and metal lures (hollow metal tube type). There are over 10,000 collectible lures all with good value. I like to pay at least $50 each for quality lures, lots more for rare ones.

**REELS** Pre-1930, bait casting type reels made of silver, German silver, bronze or black hard rubber or a combo of all of these. Up to 3" in diameter. Names: Meek, Talbot, Milam, Synder, Gayle, etc.

**BIG GAME REELS** 4" in diameter or larger, used for ocean fishing. Names to look for: E. Vom Hofe, Kovolovsky, Garey, etc.

**CATALOGS, FISH PICTURES, CREELS, EMPTY BOXES:** I like it all, collect it all, and pay you good prices for it.

### ALL BAITS PRICED ARE FOR EXCELLENT CONDITION OR BETTER. PRE-1940 BAITS

**CREEK CHUB BAIT CO. ("C.C.B.CO")**

| | |
|---|---|
| Pikie minnows | $20-100 ea. |
| Beetles | 20-50 ea. |
| Wiggle fish | 20-50 ea. |
| Sarasota | 100-200 ea. |
| Close-pin | 200 ea. |
| Ice spearing decoy | 500 ea. |
| Muskey lures | 100-300 ea. |
| Gar minnow | 150 ea. |
| Weed bug | 100 ea. |

*Shakespeare Revolution $150*

**HEDDON BAIT CO.**

| | |
|---|---|
| Underwater expert | $750 ea. |
| Slope nose | 250 ea. |
| Muskey minnow | 400 ea. |
| Black sucker | 500 ea. |
| "0" & "00" | 200 ea. |
| 100's & 150's | 5,000-200 ea. |
| Spin diver | 200 ea. |
| Light casting minnow | 150 ea. |
| Crab wigglers | 75 ea. |
| Ice spearing decoy | 300-500 ea. |
| Game fishers | 20-50 ea. |
| Tad polly | 40 ea. |
| Lung frog | 50 ea. |

| | |
|---|---|
| Vamps | 20-100 ea. |
| Torpedos | 20-75 ea. |
| Meadow mouse | 30 ea. |
| Flaptails | 25-75 ea. |
| Coast minnows | 250 ea. |

**FRED KEELING BAIT CO.**

| | |
|---|---|
| Muskey experts | $250-500 ea. |
| Flat experts | 150 ea. |
| Tom Thumb | 50 ea. |
| Muskey Tom | 50 ea. |
| Round experts | 100-200 ea. |
| Surface Tom | 50 ea. |
| Baby Clark expert | 150 ea. |

**MOONLIGHT BAIT CO.**

| | |
|---|---|
| Famous floating bait | $25 ea. |
| Trout bob | 100 ea. |
| Lady bug wiggler | 100-150 ea. |
| The "Bug" | 100 ea. |
| Dreadnought bait | 500 ea. |
| Fish nipple | 25 ea. |
| Pikaroons | 75-150 ea. |
| #3000 series | 100 ea. |
| Bass seeker | 50 ea. |

*"Heddon" Artistic Minnow $100*

**PFLUEGER BAIT CO.**

| | |
|---|---|
| Neverfail minnow | $50-150 ea. |
| Metalized minnow | 150 ea. |
| Trory minnow | 500 ea. |
| Spearing monnow | 400 ea. |
| Pak Ron minnow | 250 ea. |
| Catalina minnow | 250 ea. |

| | |
|---|---|
| Wizard minnow | 150 ea. |
| Flying helgramite | 2000 ea. |
| Surprise minnow | 100-200 ea. |
| Kent frog | 100-200 ea. |
| All-In-One | 250 ea. |
| Pal-O-Mine | 25-50 ea. |
| Bender popping minnow | 100 ea. |
| O'Boy minnow | 50 ea. |
| Weedless frog | 25-50 ea. |
| Scoop minnow | 20-40 ea. |

*Shakespeare Minnow $100*

## SHAKESPEARE BAIT CO.
| | |
|---|---|
| Revolution - wood or cork | $1000 ea. |
| Revolution hollow metal, aluminum | 10-150 ea. |
| Hydroplane | 100 ea. |
| Punkin-seed minnow | 150 ea. |
| Whirlwind spinner | 100 ea. |
| Muskey minnow | 300-500 ea. |
| Little Joe | 50 ea. |
| Barnacle Bill | 100 ea. |
| Saltwater special | 200 ea. |
| Albany floating bait | 500 ea. |
| Sardina | 200 ea. |
| Favorite floating bait | 100 ea. |
| Evolution minnow | 150 ea. |
| Tarpalunge | 100 ea. |
| Bass-A-Lure | 50 ea. |
| Rhodes mechanical frog | 100 ea. |
| Waukazoo spinner | 100 ea. |

## SOUTH BEND BAIT CO.
| | |
|---|---|
| Under-water minnows | $50-150 ea. |
| Lunge-Oreno | 100 ea. |
| Muskie casting minnows | 400 ea. |
| Gulf-Oreno | 125 ea. |
| WhirlOreno | 75 ea. |
| Plaunk-Oreno | 50 ea. |
| Vacuum bait | 100 ea. |
| Truck-Oreno | 200 ea. |
| Two-Oreno | 50 ea. |
| Bass-Oreno | 10-20 ea. |

## SMALL BAIT CO "NAMES"
| | |
|---|---|
| Abbey & Imbrie Co. | $20-100 ea. |
| Decker Bait Co. | 20-100 ea. |
| Al Foss Bait Co. | 10-50 ea. |
| Jamison Bait Co. | 20-75 ea. |
| Outing Bait Co. | 50-100 ea. |

| | |
|---|---|
| Bush-Tango Baits | 20-150 ea. |
| Wilson Bait Co. | 10-175 ea. |

*B.F. Meek reel $250*

## REELS "FRESH WATER"
| | |
|---|---|
| Billinghurst, "bird cage" style, 3" diameter | $500 ea. |
| J.A. Coxe, 2" to 4" diameter | 50-150 ea. |
| Heddon, #3-15, 3-25, 3-35, 45, 40 | 100-300 ea. |
| B.F. Meek & Sons, #2, 3, 4, 5 | 100-500 ea. |
| Meek & Milam, #1, 2, 3, 4, 5 | 200-600 ea. |
| Meek (Horton Mfg.) | 100-150 ea. |
| Meisselback, all sizes | 50-75 ea. |
| B.C. Milam, all sizes | 150-500 ea. |
| Orvis fly reel, 1874 patent | 500+ |
| Wm. Talbot, "Nevada MD," all sizes | 300-700 |

## REELS "SALT WATER"
| | |
|---|---|
| E. Vom Hofe, size 2" to 8" diameter | $200-100 |
| Kovlovsky, size 3" to 10" diameter | 500-1,500 |
| Kline, 3" to 8" diameter | 500-100 ea. |
| Garey, 2" to 6" diameter | 303-500 ea. |

*Pfleuger Trory Minnow $500*

## RODS - FRESH & SALT WATER
| | |
|---|---|
| Orvis | $100-500 ea. |
| Phillipson | 150-400 ea. |
| Granger | 100-250 ea. |
| H.L. Leonard | 150-500 ea. |
| Payne | 300-1,000 ea. |
| E.C. Powell | 200-500 ea. |
| Hardy | 150-300 ea. |
| F.E. Thomas | 200-500 ea. |
| Heddon | 100-300 ea. |

## CATALOGS
| | |
|---|---|
| Pre-1930 - rods, lures, reels, etc. | $25-250 ea. |
| Creels, the larger the better | 25-100 ea. |
| Empty boxes for: | |
| Lures | 10-100 ea. |
| Reels | 20-100 ea. |
| Fishing pictures, photos or oils | 20-1,000 ea. |

**I need a photo or Xerox™ photocopy. Group items together. No need to write descriptions, just send sharp clear photos or photocopies.**

**Prices P\*aid by:** Rick Edmisten
P.O. Box 686
North Hollywood, CA 91603
(818) 763-9406
Fax (818) 763-5974
Leave a message. I return all calls. Have a lot? Call collect.

# Breweriana, Mugs & Other Items

In the 1880's there were over 2400 breweries in operation in the U.S. With the advent of prohibition in 1919 this number dramatically dropped to zero. In 1933 with the repeal of "the great American experiment" approximately 1,000 breweries began operation. Today only a handful of major breweries survive. The advertising items of the pre-prohibition breweries are the most collectible and therefore the most valuable. These items include, but are not limited to, metal signs, paper signs, glass signs, metal trays, porcelain trays, mugs and steins, glasses, calendars, watch fobs, labels, match safes, advertising mirrors, tokens, bottles, openers, post cards. Items from the breweries after 1933 (post-prohibition) include any of the above as well as early beer cans. Beer was put in cans as early as 1935. Cans from 1935-1950 which say "Internal Revenue Tax Paid" or "Widthdrawn from Internal Revenue" are the most valuable. Also items with brewery characters such as the Hamm's bear or Budweiser's Bud Man are valuable in some cases. Also round ball type knobs with procelain or enamel inserts from the Breweries of the 1930's and 40's. Back bar plaster statues are also of interest and value.

As is the case with all collectibles, condition is the final criteria in setting value. Rusted, broken, torn and stained items have very little value unless they are one of a kind or extremely rare, and even then the value is diminished.

Budweiser mug from Busch Gardens $100

Etched glass Udermann Empire Brewery $300

## A Selection of Steins and Mugs

| | |
|---|---|
| Anheuser-Busch Mettlach stein showing Adophus Busch | $1,000 |
| Doelger with date of 1916 | 100 |
| Muessel 4/10L Mettlach | 125 |
| Louis Bergdoll 1849-1893 | 150 |
| San Antonio Brewing Assn. | 150 |
| Glass steins with porcelain inserts in pewter tops | 40-150 |
| Budweiser Collector's series | up to 300 |

## A Selection of Other Items

| | |
|---|---|
| Evansville Brewery 1900 calendar with children | $150 |
| Hamm's calendar with pretty girl | 350 |
| Kenny Park Brewery calendar with cute little girl | 250 |
| Yuengling 1896 calendar with two girls | 300 |
| Anheuser-Busch A with eagle watch fob | 75-400 |
| Anheuser-Busch match safe | 40 |
| Zang sterling silver match safe | 100 |
| Anheuser-Busch knife with stanhope | 125 |
| Tip trays approx. 4 1/2" round | 25-200 |
| Pocket mirrors showing bottle or Brewery | 40-150 |
| Brewery china | 10-100 |
| Etched glasses | 15-300 |
| Labels in old collections or sample books | 20-1000 |
| Photos of saloons which includebeer/whiskey ads | 20-50 |
| Whiskey signs/trays pre prohibition | 100-1000 up |
| Decorated whiskey back bar bottles and mugs | 50-300 |

**Photographs of the item[s] you have for sale are extremely helpful.**

# A Selection of Post Prohibition Items

| | |
|---|---|
| Apache beer can | $500 |
| Bluebonnet beer can | 200 |
| Blue Boar Ale beer can | 250 |
| Eureka beer can (3 varieties) | 100-300 |
| Gold Age beer can | 400 |
| Indian Queen Ale beer can | 1,000 |
| Leidig's beer can | 750 |
| Travis beer can | 800 |
| Plaster statue of Grand Prize Pete | 150 |
| Plaster statue of A-1 Cowboy with clock | 300 |
| Ball tap knobs | 10-200 |
| 1930's-40's tin over cardboard signs | 10-200 |
| 1930's-40's round and square trays | 10-200 |

SPECIAL NOTE – Billy and J.R. beer cans are worth only about 50¢.

## A Selection of Signs (samples of prices paid)

| | |
|---|---|
| Anheuser-Busch showing bottles on shore (metal or glass) | $3,500 |
| Anheuser-Busch Budweiser Girl metal 24"x36" | 700 |
| Alamo Girl tin 19"x 25" | 1,000 |
| Consumers paper showing goats pulling a wagon | 500 |
| Hoster paper showing large brewery | 500 |
| Jetter tin showing elk and bottle | 750 |
| Jung tin showing bottles on table family in background | 1,000 |
| Leisy's tin showing men in car with waiter bringing beer | 700 |
| Schlitz round tin showing couple in blacksmith shop | 500 |

## A Selection of Trays (samples of prices paid)

| | |
|---|---|
| Anheuser-Busch 18"x15" oval showing brewery | $700 |
| Akron 16" x 14" oval showing brewery and bottle | 500 |
| Berkshire oval showing girl riding horse | 450 |
| Breidt oval showing brewery | 750 |
| Dallas 16" oval showing flowers and bottle | 400 |
| Foss-Schneider 16" oval showing flags and medals | 500 |
| Gerst 12" round showing pretty girl with glass | 400 |
| National 16" oval showing cowboys on horseback | 1,000 |
| National 12" round showing cowboy breaking through paper | 700 |
| Northwestern 12" round showing topless Indian on buffalo | 900 |
| Ruhstallers 13" square showing man with ladies in car | 500 |
| Stroh 13" square showing Munich child with case | 600 |
| Tacoma "Anti-Katzenjammer" | 350 |

Birmingham Ideal Bottled Beer tray from Alabama  $1,000
This tray contains the two elements most sought by tray collectors:  pretty girls and labeled bottles of beer.

**Prices Paid by:**  Lynn Geyer
300 Trail Ridge
Silver City, NM  88061
(505) 538-2341      Fax  (505) 388-9000

# Cigar Boxes & Related Items

Since there are 1,500,000 brands of cigars, the brand name means little. Collectors buy most boxes for the pictures on the label. Most boxes are worth from $15 to $30, but a few bring as high as $300+.

Condition is critical in pricing a box. Boxes that are filthy or that have serious writing or water staining on the inside labels are not of interest.

Call me with boxes picturing Negroes, Chinese, baseball players or other sports, cartoon characters, political candidates, or claims to cure an ailment.

*Left: Revenue stamps before 1910 wrap around box. These are best. Right: A short 4" tax stamp means your box was made after 1917 and is less likely to be of interest.*

### A Few of the Thousands of Brands I'm Seeking:

| | | | | | |
|---|---|---|---|---|---|
| Alcazar (box in early style) | $30 | Dash little cigars | $50 | Lime Kiln Club (rare) | $300 |
| Alcazar (tin can) | 125 | Dr. Quack | 100 | Liver Regulator | 100 |
| Asthma Cure | 500 | Dr. Stork | 60 | Old Virginia Cheroots | 0 |
| Ben Bey (large tin) | 15 | Eddie Cantor | 30 |   with 1883 tax stamp | 30 |
| Bible Class cigars | 200 | Free Cuba (flag) | 40 | Our Candidates | 100-350 |
| Black Fox (tin) | 200 | Hambone | 75 | Pittsburgh Smoke (tin) | 125 |
| Brown Beauties (tin) | 200 | Health brand box | 75 | Rail Splitter (either) | 75 |
| Brown Beauties (box) | 20-50 | Health Brand (tin & paper) | 30 | Rochester Rod & Gun | 75 |
| Buster Brown (box) | 150-300 | Health Brand (litho on tin) | 100 | Sam Gompers | 30 |
| Buster Brown (tin) | 800 | Hoffman House (naked) | 125 | Temptation | 150 |
| Capadura | 25-100 | Hoffman House (clothed) | 30 | Thora (early semi-nude) | 50 |
| Cheese It (round) | 250 | Home Run stogies | 800 | Three Jackasses | 75 |
| Cure all | 100 | KKKK | 500 | White Cap ("get out") | 350 |
| Dan Patch (wood box) | 50 | Lime Kiln Club (common) | 125 | Women's Rights | 350 |

### Specific Brands with Little Value:
### These Wooden Boxes Are Usually Worth $3 or Less

| | | | |
|---|---|---|---|
| 44 | Dime Bank | Juan de Fuca | Reynaldo |
| 1886 | Dixie Maid | King Edward | RG Dun |
| 7-20-4 | Donalda | La Corona made in US | Robt. Burns after 1901 |
| Admiration | Dunhill | La Fendrich | Roberts |
| Alhambra | Dutch Masters | La Palina | Roi Tan |
| Antonio y Cleopatra | El Producto | La Primadora | Rum Soaked |
| Aurelia | El Sidelo | La Yerba | San Felice |
| Back & Co. | El Trellis | Little Fendrich | Sano |
| Bances | El Verso | London Whiffs | Santa Fe |
| Bayuk Ribbon | Emanello | Lovera | Spencer Morris |
| Belinda | Factory Seconds | M. & O. | Swann |
| Benson & Hedges | Factory Smokers | M. Ibold | Swisher Sweets |
| Bering | FactoryThrowouts | Mark IV | Tampa Nugget |
| Bock y Ca. made in US | Garcia Grande | Marsh Wheeling | Te Amo |
| Bold | Garcia, Jr. | Monogram | Thompson & Co. |
| Brooks & Co. | Garcia y Vega | Muniemaker | Tiona |
| Chancellor | Gold Label | Muriel | Tom Keene |
| Chas Denby | Habanello | Optimo | Top Stone |
| Charles Thomson | Hav-A-Tampa | Osan | Tudor Arms |
| Cinco | Havana Ribbon | Partagas after 1917 | Tufuma |
| Corina | Have A Sweet | Perfecto Garcia | Van Dyke |
| Cremo | House of Windsor | Phillies | Y-B |
| Cuesta Rey after 1917 | Humo | Pippens | Webster |
| Cuesto | H.Upmann after 1917 | Ramon Allones | White Owl |
| Del Cara | John Ruskin | Red Dot | Wolf. Bros. |

**Boxes after 1945 have no value, except very unusual ones.**
**Foreign boxes, except Canadian, almost never have value.**
**Ordinary Cuban boxes made after 1917 are worth $1; earlier $10 up.**

# Boxes with These Labels are Wanted

| | | | | |
|---|---|---|---|---|
| Famous Indian chiefs | $40-75 | Political candidates | $40-250 |
| Other Indians | 30-50 | KKK themes | 200+ |
| Cowboys, generic | 50-200 | Cartoon characters | 30-300 |
| Famous badmen | 100-150 | Winnie Winkle | 10+ |
| Buffalo Bill pre 1901 | 250 | Yellow Kid (in color) | 200 |
| Movie cowboys | 50-100 | Buster Brown | 150-300 |
| Movie stars | 30-100 | Mutt & Jeff | 50 |
| Negro racism | 60-300 | Maggie & Jiggs | 250 |
| Chinese racism | 75-300 | Gambling, high life | 20-50 |
| Baseball | 100-300 | Bicycle riding | 50-100 |
| Joe Tinker | 150 | Puns and jokes | 20-50+ |
| Cy Young | 850 | Weddings | 30+ |
| Other named players | 100+ | Uncle Sam | 50-75+ |
| Other sports | 30-100 | Men at work | 20-50 |
| Race horses, specific | 30-75 | Women in "men's" occupations | 30-75 |
| Fishing | 20-40 | Fairs & Expos | 30-100 |
| Boxing | 50-150 | Special events | 30-100 |
| Railroad trains | 20-60 | Policemen | 20-50 |
| Overland (early) | 10 | Firemen | 30-75 |
| Overland (snowbound train) | 75 | Other civil servants | 20-50 |
| Christmas | 20-40 | Children smoking | 30-50 |
| Santa Claus | 75-125 | Religious figures | 20-50 |
| Other holidays | 50-75 | Women's rights, voting | 100-200 |
| Nudes | 50-100 | Animals doing human things | 20-40 |
| Risque (naughty) | 100-300 | Maps of cities, counties, etc. | 20-50 |
| XXX rated (explicit) | 750 | Presidents of the U.S. | 20-100+ |

## Other Styles of Boxes Wanted

- Book shaped boxes are $20-30, but great labels can make them $100 up.
- Boxes in unusual shapes like mailboxes, railroad cars, game boards, bottles, and the like will usually bring from $75-$250.
- Large floor standing chests are worth from $300 to $700 or more.
- Tin cans, valued between $15 and $500. Near mint condition only.

## Other Items Related to Cigars

**Label catalogs:** value ranges from $100 to as much as $1,000 or more, depending on the printer, number of labels, age and subject matter.

**Photos of factories and stores:** photos bring from $20 to $40 with a few bringing more, depending on subject matter. Want interiors, exteriors, salesmen, delivery wagons, box factories, lithographers, etc.

**Books listing factories and addresses:** Trade directories from 1860 to 1930 will bring at least $100 each. A few years will bring more.

**Cigar band collections** are of interest if the bands are pictorial and fine condition. Values are from 1¢ to $1 each, with pictorial sets bringing more. Must be seen.

**Musical instruments made from cigar boxes:** Value ranges from $75 to $150 depending on the workmanship, condition and style.

**Other items made from boxes** will be considered.

**Paintings of cigar boxes:** Value is $125 up, with most under $500.

---

**Prices Paid by:** Tony Hyman
Box 3000
Pismo Beach, CA 93448
(805) 773-6777   Fax: (805) 773-8436   thyman@tobacciana.com
Make a Xerox™ copy of the inside lid of a box you wish to sell. It is helpful if you also copy the bottom and the end with a pictorial label. If the box is full of cigars, don't disturb them. If the box is an unusual shape, take a photograph. All mail answered if you include an SASE. Handbook of American Cigar Boxes, a 176p hardcover book that teaches you how to evaluate boxes, complete with up to date price guide is available on sale for only $23.95.

# Cigarette Lighters

### FIRE MAKING DEVICES, RELATED ITEMS & INFORMATION

Lighters have been associated with tobacco for more than three centuries. Making fire goes back further than can be imagined. The history of these subjects and the contrivances that have been conceived are of interest to me.

### Prices determined by desirability, age, scarcity & condition

A gold Dunhill watch lighter new in the box with instructions may be worth several thousands of dollars, but in the poorest condition has little value more than its gold content. On the other hand, a 17th century flintlock tinderbox in any condition may also be quite valuable if it is one of only a couple examples known to exist. Generally speaking, the value of modern lighters is affected most by dings, scratches and other wear that comes from use and whether it is complete or missing parts. Call me if you have any questions about lighters.

### Call me collect if you have:

| | | | |
|---|---|---|---|
| Any Dunhill lighters in gold or silver, with watches especially. | | Column | $1,000+ |
| | | Jet | 300+ |
| Dunhill hidden watch in gold | $3,000+ | Ruler | 200+ |
| | | Bell | 300+ |
| Other Dunhills include: | | Roman Lamp | 300+ |
| The Book Lighter | 300+ | Ball in sterling or gold | 300+ |
| The Hunting Horn | 400+ | Silent Flames | 30-1,000+ |
| Tintrol | 1,000+ | Aquariums | 500+ |

- Table and pocket lighters, *except* rectangular pocket lighters made during the 1950's and later unless they have a watch or other special feature built in

- Roll-A-Lite models are worth a little more than the gold content to me

- Any quality gold, silver or enamel lighters: Clark, Eterna, Boucheron, Van Cleef and Arpells, Boucheron, Cartier, Tiffany, and Asprey models made in the 1920's, 30's and 40's). These can bring      up to $5,000

- Ronson lighters built into picture frames, incense burners, bookends, inkwells, etc., marked A.M.W., Art Metal Works or L.V.A.    $50-250

- Pre-1900 lighters or devices for making fire are my favorite    $100+

- Unusual figural lighters of artistic appeal made during the first    $75+
  half of the 20th century or before

- Art deco designs, whether pocket or table models, uncommon Evans, Elgin American, Lincoln, Kum-A-Part, Myon, Hermes, Lancel, Transfo, brass trench lighters, Parker, Beney, McMurdo, Bruma, Thorens, Golden Wheel, Swank, Abdulla, Austrian Spelter, Ronson figural, or those marked Occupied Japan    $50-500+

- Zippos with square corners or the hinge soldered to the outside of the case    $300+

- Zippos with Disney characters, political and tobacco ads    $25+

- Cigarette case and lighter combinations in near to mint condition are wanted, especially those with watches and compact made by Ronson, Marathon, Evans and other companies    $20-3,000

- Any books, catalogs, photos or people using anything depicting making fire, sparks, friction, advertisements, ads or items such as punch boards, etc.    $10-500

For brands and models not listed please inquire. Lighters without a brand name or markings may still be of interest to me. Photos are most helpful when asking for specific information. Entire collections may be of interest for purchase. No one will pay higher prices than I will for things I don't have.

- Items from the 17th, 18th and 19th centuries that I don't have.
- Items with flint and tinder.
- Chemical bottles with mechanical devices attached to them.
- Early matches from the mid to beginning of the 19th century.
- Devices that used caps or gun powder.
- Solar devices whether pocket or table models.    $20-10,000 for the best of this category (see photo)

Verbal appraisals of single pieces and entire collections are available for a reasonable fee. Twenty two years experience and continuing. Send a stamped self addressed envelope. Include your telephone number

| **Prices Paid by:** | Tom O'Key |
| | P.O. Box 504 |
| | Anaheim, CA 92815 |
| | (714) 630-8919    Fax (714) 632-8275 |

# Cowboy Collectibles

Ranch gear, rodeo, movie, vaquero and wild west shows can all be considered Cowboy Collectibles. The ranges given are for items made before WWII (1940) in good condition with original parts. Outstanding examples will go beyond these prices in certain markets. We stay flexible and approachable. Although the best is sought, everything is considered. If in doubt, call.

| | |
|---|---|
| Boots, early, pre 1940s with color | $40-100 |
| Buckle Sets, Silver Ranger Sets | 35-75 |
| Cuffs, leather, maker marked | 85-200 |
| Cuffs, leather, unmarked | 40-100 |
| Gauntletts, maker marked | 50-100 |
| Hats, big 5" brim, worn | 40-80 |
| Hats, J.B. Stetsons pre 1930 | 40-200 |
| Photos, working cowboy in studio | 15-35 |
| Scarves, silk with cowboy scene | 20-50 |
| | |
| Chaps, leather, unmarked | $85-350 |
| Chaps, leather, maker marked | 200-500 |
| Chaps, decorated with conchas | 500-1,000 |
| Chaps, "Woolie", good condition | 400-1,000 |
| Reatas, braided rawhide | 75-200 |
| Reins, braided rawhide | 75-200 |

Saddles, sterling silver mounted, with maker marks
such as Bohlin or Visalia: $1,000
Military Saddles 100-200
Saddle Company Catalogues pre-1940
Names to look fo: Bohlin, Coggshall,
R.T. Frazier, Furstnow, S.C. Gallup,
Hamley Heiser, Main & Winchester,
Padgett Brothers, Porter, Visalia and others

Holster and gun belts, maker marked, old
**No guns!!** $75-500

Horsehair work: hitched & braided-old
Bridles with reins, complete $200-2,000
Belts with buckles 30-200
Hat bands (not new from Mexico) 20-100
Quirts, multi-colored 50-350

## Spurs

Names to look for: J.O. Bass, Crocket, G.S. Garcia, Kelly Bros., McChesney, Ricardo, and those marked with a star or anchor. No Far East Imports Please!

| | |
|---|---|
| Spurs, plain iron, pre-1930's | $75-200 |
| Spurs, Silver Mounted | 100-1,000 |
| Old Mexican Silver Mounted Spurs | 50-200 |
| Spur Straps, old leather | 15-50 |
| Spur Straps, Maker Marked | 50-100 |

$350

$650

$175

$350

---

**Prices Paid by:** Lee Jacobs
P.O. Box 3098
Colorado Springs, CO 80934
(719) 473-7101

# Horse Bits

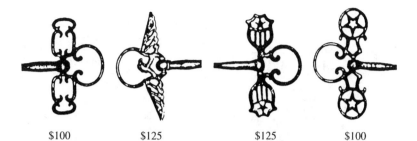

$100         $125         $125         $100

| | |
|---|---|
| Bits, silver mounted riding bridle bits | $100-1,000 |
| Bits, old iron, driving and riding | 5-30 |
| Bits, U.S. military, pre 1900 | 75-500 |
| Bits, fancy driving, w/intricate cheeks | 25-125 |

# Tin Tags

**TOBACCO TIN TAG TRADING CENTER USA**
sTagger Lee Jacobs
P.O. Box 3098
Colorado Springs, CO 80934
(719) 473-7101

**Collections purchased.** Criteria for evaluating include condition, color, age, subject and rarity.
**Small collections** under 500 tags, receive less per tag than large collections over 1000 tags.
This is because large collections are more likely to have rare and unusual tags in them.

| | |
|---|---|
| Small collections | $1 or less per tag |
| Large collections | up to $4 per tag |

**Individual tags** – Blacks, political, war related, ladies and sports tags bring premium prices   50¢-$75

| **Examples of rare tags** | | |
|---|---|---|
| | Slide Kelly Slide (baseball) | $60-80 |
| | Saturday Night (nudes) | 75-100 |
| | Cosby's Hambone (black) | 35-60 |
| | War Cry (war) | 25-30 |

$15         $15         $10         $20

# Old Photos

Photos are an interesting look back at our past, which most people collect by topic. I am interested in any photo of any place in the world before WWII. Below is a very general guide to prices paid. Some items command even higher prices than listed.

CIVIL WAR:

| | |
|---|---|
| Full Soldier | 15-100 |
| Scenes | 25-250 |

STEREO VIEWS:

| | |
|---|---|
| Cowboys | 15-150 |
| Indians | 25-250 |
| Civil War | 20-200 |

DAGUERREOTYPES:

| | |
|---|---|
| Small | 20-100 |
| Large | 50-500 |

CABINET CARDS: (4″ x 6″)

| | |
|---|---|
| Portraits | 3-100 |
| Scenes | 20-200 |
| Cowboys | 15-150 |
| Indians | 45-300 |

CDVS: (2.5″ x 4″)

| | |
|---|---|
| Portraits | 2-100 |
| Scenes | 15-250 |
| Cowboy | 20-200 |
| Indians | 50-300 |

POSTCARD REAL PHOTO:

| | |
|---|---|
| Street Scenes | 5-40 |

OTHER PHOTOS:  3-100

Please remember, both the condition and quality of a photo help determine price. When making an inquiry give a good written description, send a good photo copy, or if sending original, send it insured. Any story that goes with photo may help price.

*Left: Indian aquitted of murder in 1892. $200.*
*Above: Small western So. Dak. town postcard. $35.*

*Mr. Kolbe is currently co-authoring a book about Photographers who worked in Dakota Territory, No. Dak. and So. Dak. before 1920. Any help would be appreciated. Other photo history books are planned.*

| **Prices Paid by:** | Robert Kolbe |
|---|---|
| | 1301 South Duluth |
| | Sioux Fall, SD 57105 |

# Indian Artifacts

- **Stone Items** - arrowheads, spearheads, stone axes, celts, pipes, ceremonial pieces, gorgets, bannerstones, etc. Will pay up to $5,000 for good birdstones or other items.

- **Baskets** - Apache, California, Pomo, Northwest coast, Pima, Eskimo, etc. Basket must be in good condition. Will pay up to $5,000 for one basket.

- **Weavings** - Navaho, Satillo serapes. Will pay up to $5,000.

- **Bone, Shell & Wood** - Eskimo, Northwest coast, awls, effigies, wood carvings, rattles, bone or ivory, boxes, wood masks or items. Will pay up to $5,000 for items.

- **Beadwork** - Awl bags, possible bags, knife sheaths, bandolier bags, dolls, pipe bags, mirror cases. Any type of beadwork. Will pay up to $5,000 for one item.

- **Pipe Tomahawks** - Cast iron or brass tomahawk heads. Prefer with original handles, knife blades, staffs. Will pay up to $5,000 for one item.

- **Pottery** - Acoma, Hopi, Pueblo, Zia or Zuni. Will pay up to $2000 for one item.

*Arrowpoints and knives are evaluated on size, workmanship, material, attractiveness and authenticity.*

(A) Drill points from the Midwestern US, 300 AD to 1500 AD; eight illus: $20-200
(B) Archaic Thebes point, 200 BC to 500 AD, 4" long ($100); Longer lengths: to $1,500
(C) Hardin barb,Mississippi River, 100 BC-500 AD 4" long ($100); Longer lengths: to $1,000
(D) Big knife from Mississippi River, 1000 BC to 1200 AD. One of desired shapes for these; other configurations can bring $500+
(E) Dixon points, Illinois, 1000 BC-1000 AD $100

(F) Dalton, Mississippi River, 8000 BC to 6000 BC (also called "early man" or "paleo points") at 3" long brings $100
(G)Hopewell corner notch, Illinois, Ohio, Indiana 1000 BC to 500 AD $100
Longer lengths up to $1,000
(H)Birdstone, Midwest, 4000 BC to 1000 BC $2,000
(I) Pipe tomahawks, circa 1800's, must have original head & handle up to $5,000

**I am only interested in items that have been obtained legally and not off of any state or federal lands, national forests or from any other areas deemed protected and which it is illegal to remove Indian artifacts.**

**Please feel free to call or list what you have and make a drawing, Xerox or send a picture giving all measurements. Include your home and work phone numbers.**

| Prices Paid by: | Jan Sorgenfrei | |
|---|---|---|
| | 10040 State Route. 224 West | (419) 422-8531 days |
| | Findlay, OH 45840 | Fax (419) 422-5321 |

# Boy Scout Patches

Since the beginning of the Boy Scouts of America in 1910, scouts of all ages have collected scouting memorabilia. Over the years, the primary focus has shifted from the acquisition of entire uniforms from scouts of other countries to the collecting of primarily U.S. patches, medals and neckerchiefs. The area of strongest interest, and therefore value, is Order of the Arrow. These patches almost always have 3 W's (WWW) and the number of the lodge. The Order of the Arrow is an honor brotherhood in scouting founded in 1915 and early items of memorabilia are much sought after. Even more recent O.A. patches bring $2.50 each compared to pennies for less collected local events such as camporees and Scout-o-Ramas. Prices quoted are always for mint, unused patches. A good, used patch will usually bring 50% of the price for a new one. I prefer to buy entire collections and accumulations, but will of course buy individual patches I need. Patches I buy go into a display which you might see one day at a scouting event. Patches I already have or cannot fit into my collection, usually find their way into the collections of other scouters across the country. Following is a listing of SOME of the items I buy:

- **ORDER OF THE ARROW** patches from all years, the older the better.
  Example: Lodges 155 Michikinaqua, 219 Calusa, 246 Wakoda, and 538
    Baluga Lodge will bring you $1,000 each. Lodges 47 Hanigus,
    154 Checote, 177 Victorio, 543 Monsey, 311 Koo Ben Sho,
    182 Lone Wolf, and 370 Massassoit will bring $500 each.
  Any Order of the Arrow lodge patch $2.50 each.

- **NATIONAL JAMBOREE** staff items and arm bands, the older the better.
  Example: 1953 and 1957 O.A. Service Troop arm bands - $500 ea. 1953
    Jamboree staff jacket patch with "California" below wagon - $300

- **WORLD JAMBOREE** items, the older the better.
  Example: 1924 World Jamboree, flag-shaped, serially numbered,
    official silk patch is worth $2,000. The 1933, 1937, and 1947 World
    Jamboree official patches will bring you $250 each.

- **BSA MEDALS AND AWARDS,** pre-1950.
  Example: First Honor Medal in gold is $1,000.

- **RANKS AND INSIGNIA,** pre-1940.
  Example: Original Eagle medals 1912-15 with the eagle made of bronze
    or brass - $1,000 ea. Ranger medal $300, Ace medal $500.

- **WORLDS FAIR SERVICE CORPS,** pre-1964.
  Example: 1933 Worlds Fair Service Corps patch or neckerchief: 150 ea.

- **BADGES & COLLAR PINS OF OFFICE**, especially national level.
  Example: First International Commissioner patch is worth $500 each.
    First National Scout Commissioner patch is $250 each.

- **NATIONAL ORDER OF THE ARROW CONFERENCE.**
  Example: 1927 wallet worth $500, 1927 celluloid pin worth $1,000,
  1933 celluloid pin worth $1,000, 1936 Leader ribbon worth $400,
  1940 medal with ribbon and name bar worth $500, 1940 staff
  neckerchief worth $400, and 1975 arm bands at $50 each.

- **ORDER OF THE ARROW NATIONAL COMMITTEE** official items
  Example: Red felt vigil sash for committee members worth $2,000.
  Red cloth sash issued for 75th Anniversary of OA is $500.

- **FELT ORDER OF THE ARROW SASHES.**
  Example: Original white arrow on black felt sash is $750. Red on white
  felt vigil sash with triangle in center of the arrow is $250.

- **NATIONAL ORDER OF THE ARROW CONFERENCE CONTIN-
  GENT ISSUES**
  Example: Neckerchiefs issued by lodges for their contingent to the
  NOAC will bring $25 each. Beaded flaps issued for NOAC's are
  $50 each. Many other contingent pieces have a strong premium.

- **CHENILLE OA PATCHES**
  Example: These are patches made like High School letters with the
  wool raised loops sometimes called "rugs". Any chenille is worth
  $20. An original from Packanke or Eriez Lodges is worth $500.

- **REGION PATCHES**
  Example: patches from the original 12 Regions are only worth $3-5 ea.
  This is the biggest change in value and surprise for the "old-timers".
  Since the change in regions (now to only 4), the value has been lost.
  Still valuable however are the early felt Region patches: R5-$100,
  R8-$200, R9-$100, R12-$100

- **PHILTURN ROCKY MOUNTAIN SCOUT CAMP**
  Example: patches (originals) will bring $200 each.

- **COUNCIL SHOULDER PATCHES (CSP'S)**
  Example: Kootaga reverse colors, Nevada purple dollar, Washington
  Trails fleur de lis, and Okefenokee "stars and bars" are all $500 ea.
  Any CSP's are worth 75¢ each in quantity.

- **PATROL MEDALLIONS**
  Example: Round without "BSA" are $20 ea. Square ones bring $75 ea.

- **MERIT BADGES**
  Example: Old square merit badges $6 each if mint, $2 each if used.

- **CAMP PATCHES**
  Example: Pre-1960 cloth are worth $1 each. Felt ones are $2 each.

- **CAMPOREES, SCOUT-O-RAMAS, SCOUT CIRCUS, AND
  OTHER LOCAL ISSUES**
  These essentially have no value except in the town that issued them and
  even then they sell for a very small amount.

The very best way to show me what you have is to Xerox™ the patches. You can
usually get 8-10 patches on a page. From that copy (black and white is fine) I can
tell what issues you have, the condition of the patches and be better able to discuss
prices with you. In advance, I'd like to thank you for any help that you can give me.

| **Prices Paid by:** | Dr. Ronald G. Aldridge | (940) 455-2519 eves |
| | 250 Canyon Oaks Drive | (940) 455-5094  fax |
| | Argyle, TX  76226 | pnpsparty@aol.com |

# Marine Antiques

The following categories are too subjective and complicated to reduce to average price ranges. Each of your items must be considered on a per item basis. It is impossible to accurately estimate value without seeing an item in person. Items range from $100 to more than $10,000. This page is to inform you of items which are more readily sellable and to offer my services when you are ready.

## We are interested in memorabilia in the following categories:

### SCRIMSHAW
Scrimshaw is work done by whalemen during the era of whaling, perhaps including the work of retired or shorebound whalemen. We are only interested in 19th century antique items, particularly American, Australian, English and Dutch material. We do not buy contemporary work, reproductions, or items of questionable age.

**Sperm whale teeth** decorated with whaling or other types of scenes;
**Whalebone furniture**, pie crimpers or jagging wheels;
**Swifts or yarn winders**, and other tools, toys or household implements;
**Inlaid boxes.**

### HALF HULL MODELS
Before blueprints sectional, scale models were constructed as practical guides for building ships. Since both sides of a ship are the same only a half was made. Some were later painted or mounted and given to owners or used as designs. We buy original pieces, primarily American but also models in mirrored glass cases, clipper ships, merchant and whaling vessels, as well as yachts, both power and sail.

### SHIP MODELS
We seek 18th, 19th and early 20th century models of quality, especially planked models in original paint and decoration. Except in extraordinary circumstances we do not want Spanish galleons, Chinese junks, the Mayflower, Viking ships, Mississippi riverboats, or anything made of plastic or fiberglass.

We are interested in the following types of ship models in almost any condition. Since we restore them, broken models are acceptable, but of lesser value.

**American clipper ships** identified or anonymous: Flying Fish, 19th century, in fine condition, $1500; Flying Cloud in good condition, 19th century, $350; Great Republic, 19th century kit, $100

**Whaleships** (American or other) including contemporary factory ships as well as whaleboats, particularly made of bone: Wanderer, early 20th century, sailor made, $850; Morgan, early 20th century, $550; Alice Mandel 19th century, planked, $1500; Azorian Whaleboat, 20th century, made of bone, $700; Whaleboat, late 19th or early 20th century, made of bone, $1000;

**Yacht models, both sail and power:** Foam, 19th century schooner yacht, $1500; Cutter, circa 1885, $500; Topsail sloop, circa 1885, $650; wrecked sloop, circa 1880, $175; cabin cruiser, circa 1930, $400;

**America's Cup Defenders & Challengers:** America, 19th century, $850; America, 20th century kit wrecked $150; Volunteer, 19th century, $1000; Columbi,a 19th century wrecked, $450;

**Steam Yachts:** unidentified, circa 1910, $750; unidentified wreck, circa 1890, $500;

**Sidewheel Steamers:** Portland, 20th century kit, $450; Nantasket, 19th century, fine planked, $2000; unidentified wreck, $250;

**Actual Sailing Models** Marblehead class, circa 1930, mahogany planked, $850; sloop, circa 1880, $950; sloop, circa 1938, planked, $650; wreck, circa 1930, $250; wreck, circa 1900, $175; wreck, 1940, $75;

**Merchant Sailing Ships:** 19th century American ship, planked $1200; 19th century American ship, solid hull, $450; early 20th century kit, $350; 19th century wreck, $150; 20th century wreck, $100.

**NAVIGATIONAL INSTRUMENTS:** backstaff, sextants and octants made prior to 1900.

**GLOBES ON STANDS** made before 1900.

**TELESCOPES** that are tripod mounted, multi-sided, presentation or unusual.

**U.S. LIFE SAVING & LIGHTHOUSE SERVICE MEMORABILIA** including medals, life-guns, clocks, logs, buttons, uniforms, photos, and virtually all else.

**MARINE CLOCKS:** striking, Chelsea & Howard 10" diameter or large, presentations, but virtually all. Seth Thomas clocks with outside strikers only.

**MARINE PAINTINGS:** American, mostly 19th century, but some 20th, by the usual group of Bradford, Buttersworth, Drew, Gifford, Jacobsen, Lane, & Salmon. We discretely buy and broker important works.

**MARINE CHINA:** Boston mails, steamship, ocean liner, yacht and yacht club, commemorative American clippers and yachting.

**AMERICA'S CUP MEMORABILIA,** especially "J" boats from the 1930's as well as anything pre-1910.

**ALL YACHTING MEMORABILIA,** both sail and power.

**ANYTHING PERTAINING TO NANTUCKET,** including Nantucket baskets.

## WHALING LOG BOOKS & JOURNALS

Particularly American, but whaling items of any nationality are sought. Condition is important along with illustrations, whalestamps, and incidents in the voyage. Boring, routine trips are less interesting.

## MARINE LIBRARIES AND VINTAGE PHOTOGRAPHS

We aggressively buy American and British vintage marine photography as well as marine books from single volumes to complete libraries in fine condition. We do not buy naval material after 1900.

## SIGNED OR UNSIGNED IMAGES OF THE FOLLOWING:

American harbor scenes in Boston, New York, San Francisco, Newport, or Nantucket; Also images of Whaling, Yachts (sail, steam & power), Schooners, launchings, shipbuilding, sailing craft with more than 3 masts, Grand Banks fishing schooners, unusual small craft, identified ship Captains, and of folks engaged in marine occupations such as sailmakers and fishermen.

## WE HAVE PURCHASED THE FOLLOWING IN THE PAST YEAR:

Log Book Helen Augusta of Newport 1850-1854. Complete voyage to the Arctic: $2000;
Log Book Ship Louisiana of New Bedford 1853-1857. Complete voyage to the Pacific: $2200;
Log Book Black Eagle of New Bedford 1866-1867. Complete voyage to Hudson's Bay: $500;
Log Book Rosewell King of New London 1880-1881. Sea-elephant voyage to Desolation Island: $500;
Log Book John R. Manta of New Bedford 1908-1910. Partial journal in the Atlantic, along with 4 shipboard account books for other whalers: $650;
Ship's Papers of the Bark Anaconda of New Bedford 1856-1860 with papers from the schooner George Brown of Boston 1866-1868: $250.

*Scimshawed whale's tooth, polychromed, 19th C., with potrait of Alwilda, female priate,$2,000.*

*Whalebone tope turn cane 19th C., $1,000.*

*American whaleship, planked with some whalebone parts in old finish, 19th C., $1,000.*

*Tiger maple box inlaid with ebony, baleen and whalebone with fitten interior, 19th C., $1,350.*

We rarely buy marine material made, written, or printed after 1900.

**Prices Paid by:** Andrew Jacobson
Marine Antiques
Box 2155
South Hamilton, MA 01982 (508) 468-6276

# Tokens, Medals, etc.

$1,250 up for Indian Peace Medals          $1,000 up for Slave Tags

If YOU are interested in getting the best price for your tokens, medals, badges, ribbons, pin-back buttons, advertising mirrors, World's Fair collectibles, Franklin Mint issues, Masonic items and similar small collectibles, I am BUYING all types and quantities. I collect many areas, and have thousands of collectors wanting to buy your material. We also accept better material for auction. A sample copy of our recent mail bid sale catalog (color cover, almost $200,000 in sales) is available for only $9 postpaid, and includes the prices realized. We prefer items worth $15 each and up for auction. If you are interested in consignment, please send a brief description of your material and a S.A.S.E. for full information. Collectors, please write!

**SELLING:** Please SHIP for my top offer for your material. As condition does make a significant difference on price on many items, we really do prefer to see your material prior to making a firm offer. If you absolutely must have an estimate prior to shipment, send an S.A.S.E. and clear photocopies and/or descriptions for my general estimate. Due to the number of inquiries, I am unable to devote much time to price solicitations, and regret it is impossible to offer the best price from your photocopy or listing. I really do want to buy ALL of your material, and encourage you to ship for my top offer. Prices listed here are generally for the most common item and should be considered minimums. We do pay more for better items.

## COMMON MATERIAL

While I will buy all quantities, many items are extremely common to me, and are often thought to be worth substantially more by the uninformed. Some rarities do exist in some of these categories, and I am most interested in scarce to rare items. Prices shown are for nice, undamaged condition, items delivered. Write if you have large quantities. I SELL all of these items at modest prices, in quantities of 100 or more (send S.A.S.E. for price list):

| Type | Number Made | Price Paid for Common |
|---|---|---|
| Sales Tax Tokens | Several BILLION | 3¢ |
| OPA red/blue tokens | 3 BILLION | 1¢ |
| Transportation | Usually 100,000 up | 5¢ (up to 10 of each) |
| Video arcade | Millions made | 1¢ |
| Wooden nickels | Usually 1000 of each | 5¢ |
| Shell "Presidents" | Millions made | 3¢ |

Common transportation tokens are the dime and quarter sized pieces, often with cut-outs. A very few of this type are worth more. I *sell* 100 different, all metal transit tokens for $22.50, and 2500 mixed for $99.95 postpaid (in stock, just send a check). Rare transit tokens have horse-cars, or state GOOD FOR ROUND TRIP, HOTEL-DEPOT, or similar and are worth from $10 up to $1500 each. Please Ship!

## SCARCE TO RARE MATERIAL

I am much more interested in buying scarce to rare items, and will pay my best price for them. Due to the huge numbers of items issued, I can only list minimum prices for each category. Some sample prices paid for better items are also listed. I am the top buyer for all better tokens, medals, etc. To get the best price for your items, ship today!

• **Trade Tokens** ("Good For" something): I will pay $1 to $10+ for each metal trade token needed (small towns, mostly), more for smaller and western states. Paying 35¢ each and up for common pieces in small quantities, for those with a city and state. Large quantities wanted (send sample and quantity). I am BUYING all U.S. and world tokens at highly competitive prices. Collections and hoards are wanted.

• **Saloon Tokens** (MUST have the word "Saloon" on the token). I will pay at least $13 each for virtually all early Saloon tokens, more for Western states, more for pieces with pictorials, etc. I will pay $75 for a Rockford IL area Saloon, and will pay $30 up for any Illinois or Wisconsin Saloon token I need ($20 for most duplicates). Paying $50 up for "A.T." or "I.T." tokens. Also buying bar, tavern, coal and lumber tokens. Ship!

• **Hard Times–Civil War Tokens:** Will pay $4-$10 up for common pieces.

• **Dog Tags:** I will pay $25 up for pre-1901 tags; $3.50-$10 up for 1901-09; $2.50 up for 1910-19; $1.50 up for 1920-29; 75¢-$1 up for 1930-39; 35¢-50¢ for 1940-59, and 15¢-25¢ for 1960 up. Large quantities wanted (write). Seeking cat, rabies (1¢ each), other animal tags. Higher prices paid for Rockford area tags needed.

• **Civil War Dog Tags:** Paying $200 up for awarded; $500 up for named corps badges.

• **Other:** Also seeking encased coins, elongated coins, celluloid advertising, bicycle advertising & medals, Bryan Money, inaugural medals, military medals, watch fobs.

• **Credit Cards:** I've collected for 20 years, and seriously want to buy! Paying 50¢-$1 each for recent/current plastics, $2.50-$5.00 for Charge-plates, $4-$15 for metal charge tokens, up to $150 each for celluloid. Ship any quantity. Save your cards.

• **Advertising Mirrors:** All types of pocket and paperweight celluloid advertising mirrors are wanted! Paying $55-$100 up for most "Good For" mirrors. Mirrors with females, products depicted, or scenes especially wanted, most at $15-$50 up. Plain mirrors with wording only are worth $10-$25 each. Most rectangular mirrors are $1-$5 each. Ship!

• **Awarded Medals:** Any and all U.S. or world medals with hand engraving are wanted at serious prices. All gold and silver medals are wanted, especially before 1901. All other medals are also wanted. Olympic medals and souvenirs especially wanted (pre-1960). Will pay $2,500 for the 1904 Olympic medal, $3,000 if awarded with box.

• **Indian Peace Medals:** I will pay $1,250-$10,000 for genuine silver I.P. medals. Also seeking original copper medals, and all U.S. Mint issues. I wrote the PRICE GUIDE!

• **World's Fair Material:** There are so many items it is virtually impossible to list prices paid. I am most interested in pre-1940 items, but NOT in most paper, books, pamphlets or postcards (except large collections). I seek badges, pinbacks, tokens, medals, playing cards, ribbons, tickets, china, watches, letterheads, fobs, bottles, fans and all larger items, especially the unusual, awarded and engraved items, or in silver or gold.

• **Franklin Mint & Modern Mint:** All Franklin Mint medals, bars, plates, spoons, model cars and figurines are wanted at current prices. All Modern Mint issues wanted, including world proof and mint coin sets. Call today, or send SASE for Buying Guide. Will buy or auction.

• **Badges & Ribbons:** I am MOST interested in all singles and quantities of all types of plain to fancy badges and ribbons from World's Fairs ($10-100 up), G.A.R. ($2-10 up), Masonic ($.50-5 up), Confederate ($10 up), 8-hour day ($15 up), Mining related, Labor related and all other fraternal items such as banners (no uniforms or swords).

• **Chauffeur Badges:** Will pay $45 up for most early undated badges; $20 up for most pre-1920 badges; $2 each for Minnesota; $5 up for other states, with original pins.

• **Political Material:** Since condition is highly critical on pinbacks, I MUST see them prior to making any offer. Buying all types of political tokens, medals, pinbacks, china, ribbons, canes, badges, silks, etc. Please ship for my top offer. Sorry, no offers from lists.

• **Masonic & Fraternal**: All Masonic pennies, medals, badges, miniature trowels ($5-8) wanted. Paying $200 for gold pennies, $5 for silver, $2-5 up for others. Pay $50-150 for early hand engraved silver badges. Buying all fobs, pins, spoons and early china. All fraternal items *except books* wanted, especially from the Knights of Labor ($40 up!). Please ship!

• **Slave Tags:** Please call immediately! I am the highest buyer: $1,000 to $5,000

• **Dun (and Bradstreet) Oversized Commercial Directories:** Paying $100 up for pre-1901 all-state directories; $50 for 1901-20; $50 for 1921-30. Pre-1960 wanted! Ship!

• **Rockford, Freeport and Belvidere Items Wanted!** Will pay $1,500 for a mint Baier and Ohlendorf tin sign. All signs, tins, tokens, medals, badges, ribbons, etc wanted!

• **Counterstamped Coins:** With names stamped on coins: Paying $5 to $5,000 each.

• **Mining Related:** I am seriously interested in buying ribbons, badges and other items from Mining organizations: UMWofA; UMMWUofNA; WFofM; Miners Union; United Mineworkers; Eight-Hour Day, etc. Will pay $30 up for each ribbon/badge. Also buying tokens and medals, esp. early and awarded/engraved pieces. Pressed coal items wanted. Buying miner's lamps and oil wicks. *Ship!*

---

## FREE BUYING GUIDE

I offer a **FREE** 45 page Buying Guide, with minimum prices paid by category, with details of specific items I seek. Send $3 for immediate shipment, or write for a free copy when published. For the ultimate in pricing information on tokens and medals, buy the book **Identification and Values of US Tokens and Medals**, with prices, for hundreds of categories, 320 pages, illustrated. Only $22.50 postpaid. I also stock most books on tokens and medals, if you are interested in learning more, or collecting. Send two stamps for a current list.

---

I want to BUY your material. I want to buy everything in the above categories, and will do my best to make you a top offer. I purchased 99.1% of all material sent to me in 1996. I have been seriously buying since 1972, and have purchased over three million items! Don't spend the time making a list, just box it all up and ship today with your price desired, or for my very best offer. Thank You! I will travel to purchase significant collections.

| **Prices Paid by:** | Rich Hartzog | |
| --- | --- | --- |
| | World Exonumia | |
| | POB 4143 BWM | (815) 226-0771 |
| | Rockford, IL 61110 | Fax (815) 397-7662 |

# Watches

We have 33+ years experience as experts in the field of watches. We seek pocket and wristwatches, but only:

Gent's pocket watches marked 21 Jewels or more on the movement.

Historical, sports-related, gold cases, novelty character watches, and vintage (1970 or older) *better grade* wristwatches.

Also *any railroad* pocket watch.

Rolex, Patek Philippe, Howard, Illinois, Hamilton, keywinds, and any unusual watch.

Enamels, both lady's and gent's.

### HOW TO DESCRIBE YOUR POCKET WATCH:

**What condition is the watch?** Does it run and keep good time? Does *not* have to!

**Size:** If bigger than a silver dollar, it's a gent's. Smaller? Probably a lady's.

**Winding:** It's either a keywind (winds with a key) or a stemwind (winds at the top).

**What name is on the dial?**

**What is the dial made of?** Silver? Gold? White? Porcelain? Metal?

**Case:** Open face (you can see the dial without opening anything).

Hunter case (front lid covers & closes over dial).

**What is the case made of?** Gold? Silver? Silverore (base metal alloy)? *Please send a photocopy of both sides of the watch so we can see the decoration or engraving, if any, on the case.*

**Inside back lid of case:** Does it say Guaranteed 25 years (or any number of years)? If so, the case is gold filled (gold plated).

**What name is on the watch movement?**

**What serial number is one the movement?**

Numbers on the case are not important.

**Jewels:** If 21 jewels or more, this is usually marked on the watch movement. If not marked, probably less than 15 jewels. (Note: Jewels used in watch movements are worth pennies by themselves.)

*Much of the above can be useful in describing wristwatches also.*

Highest prices paid for *mint* original case, dial and movement. Prices vary according to condition and other factors.

WE DO NOT WANT any inexpensive gent's wristwatches such as Timex. We do not buy any lady's wristwatches except Patek Philippe, Rolex, Vacheron & Constantin, Audemars, Cartier. No watches after 1970.

Moonphase triple calendar gents chronograph $100+ & up

Enamel 18k pocket watch gents 18 Size Hunter $1,000+ & up

### SAMPLE PRICES PAID:

THESE ARE THE BASIC MINIMUM PRICES. MANY OF THESE ARE WORTH MUCH MORE, INTO THE THOUSANDS OF DOLLARS. PRICES VARY ACCORDING TO CONDITION, ORIGINALITY, MODEL, NUMBER OF JEWELS, CASE SIZE, DIAL, AND RARITY (OR LACK OF).

#### POCKET WATCHES

| | |
|---|---|
| Ball Official RR standard | $65+ & up |
| Hamilton 21 jewels or higher | 50+ & up |
| Illinois 21 jewels or higher | 50+ & up |
| Howard (Boston) | 35+ & up |
| Railroad pocket watch, 21 jewels+ | 45+ & up |
| Patek Philippe | 500+ & up |
| Waltham 21 jewels or higher | 35+ & up |
| Elgin 21 jewels or higher | 35+ & up |
| Repeater (chimes on command) | 250+ & up |

#### WRISTWATCHES

| | |
|---|---|
| Patek Phiiippe gent's | 650+ & up |
| Rolex gent's | 225+ & up |
| Vacheron & Constantin gent's | 250+ & up |
| Audemars Piguet gent's | 150+ & up |
| Cartier gent's | 100+ & up |

All mail answered if you send an SASE. Please include your area code and telephone number also. Make a photocopy of the front & back of the watch, and write down all the information you can see on the dial, watch movement. and inside the *back* of the case, along with all the numbers you see on the watch movement.

We pay significant finder's fees for tips leading to our purchase of collections, estates or accumulations.

---

| Prices Paid by: | Maundy International |
|---|---|
| | P.O. Box 13028-WPT |
| | Shawnee Mission, KS 66282      (800) 235-2866 toll free |

# Firearms

You can get fair prices for your guns in a way that's easy, legal and secure. *Supica's* Old Town Station, Ltd., offers **three ways to sell** your antique and collectible firearms, so you can select the one that best suits your needs.

1. Sell your collection or individual pieces outright. We usually pay 50% to 75% of retail.
2. Consign your items to our popular quarterly catalog, **Old Town Station Dispatch**.
3. Consign your items to our nationally advertised firearms specialty auctions.

However you sell through Old Town Station, Ltd., your guns are pictured in a nationally and internationally subscribed catalog sent to serious buyers and enthusiasts, listed on the World Wide Web, and advertised in national gun collector publications. Consignment rates vary from 15% to 25%. All firearms law complied with.

## Old Town Station Dispatch

Old Town Station Dispatch is a quarterly catalog and journal of antique arms with hundreds of items pictured and listed for sale in each issue. Each issue includes tips for gun collectors, along with legends and lore of the Old West. Emphasis is on antique firearms, 1850 to 1898. Subscription is $15 in the US, $35 international. Current single issue is $5. Price Guide readers may receive a free sample back issue if you send your request by mail (no phone requests for samples, please!)

## Dispatch On Line

Check out our web site at "http://members.aol.com/OldTownSta"

### ACTUAL PRICES REALIZED from a recent issue of Old Town Station Dispatch:

| | | | |
|---|---|---|---|
| Engraved Pair Presentation Colts | $35,000 | Remington Derringers | 295 to 485 |
| S & W New Model Number 3 | 450 to 1,900 | Merwin Hulbert revolvers, large frame | |
| Colt Single Action Army revolvers | | | 450 to 3,400 |
| | 850 to 4,500 | Merwin Hulbert revolvers, small frame | |
| Schofield Cavalry revolvers | 985 to 4,850 | | 235 to 650 |
| Trap & Alarm guns | 250 to 650 | Webley revolvers | 335 to 450 |
| Older air pistols | 35 to 350 | Misc. Spurtrigger revolvers | 25 to 285 |
| S&W Model 3 Amer. revolvers | 450 to 3,000 | Misc. small double action revolvers | 25 to 250 |
| Small S&W top-break revolvers | 120 to 595 | Antique Bowie knives | 50 to 1,850 |
| Small S&W tip-up revolvers | 140 to 550 | Percussion single shot pistol lrg | 385 to 1,200 |
| Engraved S&W Model Two | 3,850 | Percussion single shot pistol sml | 85 to 485 |
| S&W .357 Registered Magnum | 1,675 | Percussion rifles | 250 to 1,285 |
| Misc S&W Hand Ejector revolvers | 195 to 550 | Civil War carbines | 725 to1,150 |
| Colt 1860 Army revolvers | 785 to 1650 | Old double barrel shotguns | 195 to 2,350 |
| Colt 1849 Pocket revolvers | 350 to 1500 | Trapdoor rifles | 320 to 850 |
| Colt 1871 Open Top revolver, | | Rolling block rifles | 285 to 485 |
| carved ivory grips | 4,650 | Winchester l873's | 400 to1,200 |
| Colt 1861 Navy Conversion | 1,250 to 3,450 | Winchester 1886's | 750 to 1,100 |
| Colt 1877 Lightnings | 265 to 700 | Winchester 1895's | 650 to 895 |
| Remington 1875 revolvers | 595 to 1850 | | |

## ACTUAL PRICES REALIZED AT OUR AUCTIONS

| | | | |
|---|---|---|---|
| English breechloading caplock rifle | 5,500 | Engraved Colt Single Action Army | 4,950 |
| Japanese T-22 US trials rifle | 2,750 | Engraved Remington 1875 revolvers | |
| Japanese T-97 sniper rifles (2) | 2,090 & 1,210 | pair | 8,900 |
| Type 100 Japanese bayonet | 770 | Engraved Peabody-Martini rifle | 8,000 |
| Marlin 43 "DRG" marked shotgun | 1,045 | Colt SAA Cavalry revolver | 5,500 |

### Appraisals & consulting available.

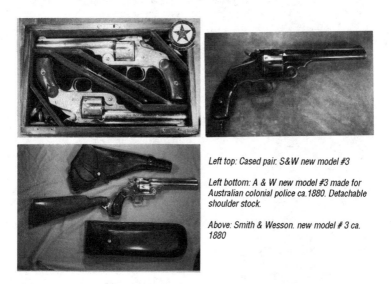

Left top: Cased pair. S&W new model #3

Left bottom: A & W new model #3 made for Australian colonial police ca.1880. Detachable shoulder stock.

Above: Smith & Wesson. new model # 3 ca. 1880

### Old Town Station, Ltd., auction & antique arms, Jim Supica, President

- Full time professional antique & collectible gun dealer & auctioneer.
- Publisher, *Old Town Station Dispatch* quarterly catalog & journal of antique arms.
- Author of articles in American Rifleman, Man at Arms, others.
- Contributing Editor, *American Rifleman* and the Blue Book of Gun Values.
- Pricing panel, *Standard Catalog of Firearms, Flayderman's Guide to Antique Arms.*
- Past President, Missouri Valley Arms Collectors Assn; Member of the Board of Directors of the Smith & Wesson Collectors Assn.
- Life Member NRA, KSRA, S&WCA, SASS. Member CADA, CCA, others.

**Standard Catalog of Smith & Wesson**: a new hardback identification & price guide co-authored by OTS President, Jim Supica, only $31.95 ppd., autographed.

| **Prices Paid by:** | Old Town Station, Ltd. |
|---|---|
| | Mail to: P.O. Box 15351 |
| | Lenexa, KS 66285 |
| | Ship to: 13400 Santa Fe Trail |
| | Lenexa, KS 66215 |
| | (913) 492-3000 for buying, selling or consigning only |
| | Fax (913) 492-3022 OldTownSta@aol.com |

# Military

## WORLD WAR TWO

### German

| | |
|---|---|
| HELMETS, ARMY | $150-800 |
| HELMETS, PARATROOPEROR "SS" | 800-3,000 |
| PARATROOPER PARACHUTE | 500-2,000 |
| ARMY DRESS DAGGER | 400-1,000 |
| "SS" OR "SA" DRESS DAGGER | 300-2,500 |
| AIRFORCE DAGGER | 300-1,000 |
| DRESS SWORD | 200-5,000 |
| FLAGS POLITICAL AND ARMY | 25-150 |
| FLAGS SPECIAL OR FANCY | 300-2,000 |
| KNIGHTS CROSS OF THE IRON CROSS | 800-2,000 |
| VARIOUS MEDALS, ARMY | 50-1,000 |
| VARIOUS MEDALS "SS" | 250-5,000 |
| ARMY VISOR HAT | 150-500 |
| ARMY M-43 CAP | 100-300 |
| ARMY COMBAT TUNIC WITH PATCHES | 250-800 |
| NAZI ARMBAND | 20-150 |
| ARMY SHIRTS / PANTS / UNDERWEAR etc. | 75-400 |
| ANY TYPE FLIGHT CLOTHING | 200-1,000 |
| AIRPLANE & VEHICLE PARTS | 100-500 |
| FIELD GEAR OF ANY TYPE | 50-1,000 |
| LEATHER JACK BOOTS | 150-300 |
| LEATHER ITEMS OF ANY TYPE | 50-1,000 |
| PLAQUES OF HITLER OR OTHERS | 150-800 |
| DOCUMENTS OF THE THIRD REICH | 25-1,000 |
| PHOTO ALBUMS | 80-250 |
| POTATO MASHER GRENADE | 100-250 |
| ANY BOMBS OR MUNITIONS (DEWAT) | 150-500 |

**We actively collect German WWII items.**

## WORLD WAR ONE

| | |
|---|---|
| U.S. OR GERMAN HELMET (COMBAT) | $50-200 |
| GERMAN SPIKE HELMET | 150-1,000 |
| DRESS DAGGER, any country | 300-1,000 |
| SWORDS | 75-500 |
| TUNICS, any country | 50-500 |
| GERMAN IRON CROSS | 45-200 |
| U.S. MEDALS & FRENCH MEDALS | 25-300 |
| AIRPLANE & VEHICLE PARTS | 50-300 |
| DOCUMENTS, any country | 20-100 |
| GERMAN FLAG | 100-500 |
| PATCHES, any country | 25-200 |
| FLIGHT ITEMS, any country | 100-2,000 |

## CIVIL WAR

| | |
|---|---|
| CONFEDERATE SWORD | $500-1,000 |
| CONFEDERATE UNIFORM | 1,000-10,000 |
| CONFEDERATE HAT | 800-3,000 |
| CONFEDERATE BELT BUCKLE | 300-2,000 |
| CONFEDERATE LETTERS OR DIARIES | 200-1,000 |
| OTHER CONFEDERATE ITEMS | up to 20,000 |
| UNION SWORD | 200-1,000 |
| UNION UNIFORM | 500-5,000 |
| UNION HAT | 300-3,000 |
| UNION BELT BUCKLE | 100-1,000 |
| UNION LETTERS OR DIARIES | 50-1,000 |
| WILL BUY ANY CIVIL WAR ITEMS | Up to 20,000 |

top: *daggers $300 - $1,000*
*spiked helmets $150 - $1,000*

middle: *swords $150 - $1,000*

bottom: *Medals $50 - $2,000*

# Military

## VIETNAM

| | |
|---|---|
| U.S. TIGER STRIPE SHIRTS AND PANTS | $100-300 |
| U.S. IN-COUNTRY MADE PATCHES | 25-300 |

*Wings $25+*

## WORLD WAR TWO
### American

| | |
|---|---|
| PARATROOPER HELMET | $500-1,200 |
| PARATROOPER JUMP JACKET | 400-1,000 |
| PARATROOPER JUMP PANTS | 350-600 |
| PARATROOPER JUMP BOOTS | 150-250 |
| PARATROOPER DRESS UNIFORM | 100-600 |
| PARATROOPER PARACHUTE | 1,000-3,000 |
| PARATROOPER ASSOCIATED ITEMS | 100-5,000 |
| FIGHTING KNIFE M-3 | 80-400 |
| K-BAR TYPE FIGHTING KNIFE | 75-200 |
| OSS FIGHTING KNIFE | 300-1,000 |
| TRENCH KNIFE | 150-300 |
| T HANDLE ENTRENCHING TOOL | 50-150 |
| HOLSTER M-1912 (45 CAL.) | 50-85 |
| HOLSTER, SHOULDER (45 CAL.) | 50 |
| OTHER HOLSTER | 25-100 |
| FLIGHT BAGS, VALISES, DUFFEL, ETC. | 25-200 |
| A-2 FLIGHT JACKET | 200-2,000 |
| FLEECE LINED FLIGHT JACKET | 100-400 |
| PARACHUTE FOR FLIGHT PERSONNEL | 800-1,500 |
| TANKER JACKET (BLANKET LINED) | 175-300 |
| M-41 LIGHTWEIGHT JACKET | 35-200 |
| IKE JACKETS, 4 POCKET TUNICS | 25-500 |
| HBT TROUSERS / SHIRT / HAT | 20-80 |
| 5 BUTTON SWEATER / JEEP HAT | 25-55 |
| BUCKLE BOOTS / SHOES / SKI BOOTS | 35-200 |
| FLIGHT GOGGLES / LEATHER HELMET | 50-200 |
| HELMET WITH LINER | 25-175 |
| MILITARY DOCUMENTS | 10-500 |
| **USMC, ARM"Y AIR CORPS., and NAVY FLIGHT ITEMS** | **Add 20-30%** |

*$400+*

*up to $2,000*

*$500+*

*$75+*

*$500+*

### Japanese

| | |
|---|---|
| COMBAT HELMET | $200-600 |
| PARATROOPER HELMET | 2,500 |
| FLIGHT SUITE | 200 |
| SAMURAI SWORD | 400-10,000 |
| COMBAT BELT / SWORD BELT | 50-200 |
| FIELD CAP | 125-200 |
| AMMO POUCHE / CLEANING KIT | 50-100 |
| COMBAT BOOTS | 100-200 |
| FIELD AND DRESS TUNICS & PANTS | 125-500 |
| RISING SUN FLAGS / MEATBALL FLAG | 25-200 |
| HOLSTERS FOR VARIOUS PISTOLS | 25-150 |
| GOGGLES | 25-150 |
| PARACHUTE FOR PARATROOPER | 800-2,000 |
| PARACHUTE FOR FLIGHT PERSONNEL | 200-1,000 |
| FIELD GEAR, anything | 100-2,000 |

*$100+*

*$150+*

We buy **anything military**, from any country or period, from the Roman Empire to Desert Storm. This is just a small listing of the items we collect and deal in. We also do **free appraisals** on any military items, if you send us a picture or call with a description of the items. Remember, there were hundreds of different armies throughout history with thousands of different types of weapons, armor, clothing and patches. So, to give a fair price on your possessions, we must have an accurate description of them.

---

**Prices Paid by:** Mike Burke
Box 20519
East York, PA 17402
(717) 699-4448     katsmilita@aol.com

---

# German WWII Souvenirs

## GERMAN DAGGERS, SWORDS & BAYONETS

| Item | Average Price | Maximum Price |
|---|---|---|
| Daggers | $100-1,500 | $25,000 |
| Swords | 150-1,000 | 5,000 |
| Bayonets | 50-500 | 1,500 |
| Hangers | 25-200 | 500 |
| Portepees (Tassels) | 15-100 | 150 |

All items must be original, pre-1945, from the manufacturer, in excellent or better condition and complete. I do not buy any reproductions. Examples of good companies are: Alcoso, Eickhorn, Holler, Horster, Weyersberg, Pack, SMF, WKC, etc. Also looking for original advertising items from these and other Solingen manufacturing firms.

*SA Brown Shirt dagger $300*

## OTHER GERMAN WAR SOUVENIRS

| Item | Average Price | Maximum Price |
|---|---|---|
| Flags | $10-100 | $150 |
| Ornate Flags | 150-500 | 3,000 |
| Helmets | 25-175 | 500 |
| Uniforms | 75-250 | 1,000 |
| Medals & Decorations | 15-200 | 1,500 |

*Iron Cross*

*$25*

Above: *Luftwaffe pilot's badge $200*

Left: *Luftwaffe standard $3,000*

**All items should be pre-1945, original, in excellent complete condition. The more ornate the better. I do not want reproductions, badly damaged items, etc. I will answer all letters and calls. I am fair, honest and have been a serious collector in this field for 35 years. I am in a position to purchase single items or entire estates.**

| **Prices Paid by:** | Lt.Col. (ret.) Thomas M. Johnson |
|---|---|
| | C/o Johnson Reference Books |
| | 312 Butler Road, #403 |
| | Fredericksburg, VA 22405 |
| (540) 373-9150 | Fax: (540) 373-0087    ww2daggers@aol.com |

# British Royalty Commemoratives

British royalty commemoratives were made for most royal occasions with the most common available from the reign of Queen Victoria through the modern-day royal family. Royal commemoratives have been issued in a wide variety of merchandise, almost anything that will take a picture and inscription. Condition is very important when pricing commemoratives. Items that are chipped, cracked, crazed, torn, or scratched are definitely lowered in value. For further reading, the book *British Royal Commemoratives* by Audrey B. Zeder is available for $27.95 postage paid from the address listed at bottom of this page.

**PRICE EXAMPLES FOR COMMEMORATIVE CERAMICS, TINS AND PRESSED GLASS IN GOOD CONDITION:**

| | |
|---|---|
| Queen Victoria | $50+ |
| Edward VII | 30+ |
| George V | 15+ |
| Edward VIII | 12+ |
| George VI | 10+ |
| Queen Elizabeth | 10+ |
| Prince Charles & Princess Diana | 8+ |

**OTHER ROYALTY COMMEMORATIVES WANTED**

| | |
|---|---|
| Bookmarks | 5+ |
| Compacts | 10+ |
| Covered boxes | 8+ |
| Egg cups | 8+ |
| Figurals | 12+ |
| Handkerchiefs | 8+ |
| Jewelry | 5+ |
| Magazines | 5+ |
| Novelties | 5+ |
| Photographs | 5+ |
| Programs | 5+ |
| Puzzles | 10+ |
| Sewing Items | 5+ |
| Tea towels | 8+ |
| Teapots | 25+ |

**COMMEMORATIVES IN THESE BRANDS ARE WANTED**

Royal Doulton, Wedgwood, Minton, Spode, Paragon

**COMMEMORATIVE EVENTS WANTED**

Coronations, Jubilees, Weddings, Anniversaries, Births, Birthdays, Visits

**Prices Paid by:** Audrey Zeder
1320 SW 10th Street #T
North Bend, WA 98045       (425) 888-6697
Send a photocopy or photograph of the items you wish to sell and a stamped self-addressed envelope for reply. Describe size, manufacturer, and any distinguishing features. It is important to describe the condition, listing any damage. **Do not send the actual item until after receiving a purchase offer.**

# Books, Prints & Paper Ephemera

## BOOKS

We buy and sell antiquarian, illustrated, medical, children's, fine press, and other types of valuable books. We have paid from $5 to $10,000. Books should be in fine condition, not damaged. We buy entire libraries of non-fiction books, but do not buy Book Club, Reader's Digest, Encyclopedias, or dictionaries after 1850.

American writers in 1st editions:
Fitzgerald, Faulkner, Hemingway,
Twain, Thoreau, Steinbeck, Cather,

| | |
|---|---|
| Welty, Parker and others | $20 - 1,000 |
| Modern European writers in 1st editions | |
| Joyce, Pound, Dickens, Dostoevski, | |
| Zola, Kafka and others | 25-1,000 |
| Antiquarian books with color plates | |
| or maps | 50-5,000 |
| Arkham House and selected other | |
| works and publishers of fantasy | 25-250 |
| Limited Edition Club books | 20-1,500 |
| Western and Indian books | 10-300 |
| Voyages and travels | 50-1,000 |
| Architecture and photography | 25-1,000 |
| Small private press books | 25-1,000 |
| Books about books, art of books | 25-1,000 |
| Medical books | |
| Prior to 1820 | 20-500 |
| Copyright 1821-1910 | 10-500 |
| Children's books | |
| 1860-1900 | 5-500 |
| 1900-1940 | 5-500 |
| 1940-1960 | 5-100 |
| Illustrated books | |
| Early *Chapbooks* and other 18th | |
| and 19th century illustrated | 20-5,000 |
| *Harpers Weekly* bound annuals | 100-350 |

## PAPER EPHEMERA

We buy and sell paper ephemera, trade catalogs, Shaker labels, legal documents, and historically interesting or graphically attractive paper items of all sort. All items must be in fine condition. We will buy complete collections or important singles.

| | |
|---|---|
| Shaker labels | $10-50 |
| Trade catalogs | 10-1,000+ |
| Legal documents 18th century | 10-300 |
| Legal documents 19th century | 10-200 |
| Legal documents about slavery | 5-200 |

## PRINTS

We buy and sell printed graphic arts and maps, especially hand colored, florals, birds, Indians, atlases and modern limited editions by famous artists. All items must been in good condition.. The value depends upon the artist, size, and subject matter. The range is from $50 to $2,500

| | |
|---|---|
| Currier & Ives | 20-3,000 |
| McKinney Hall Indians | 50-200 |
| Thomas Hart Benton | 100-500 |

## AUTOGRAPHS

We buy and sell autographs and documents signed by the famous and infamous. Values can range from as low as $5 to as much as $100,000 for a single item. A selection of values is given here for your information, but every document must be evaluated as to the importance of its content, condition, scarcity, author and demand. Hand written letters with important content are usually the most valuable. Other letters, typed letters, signed forms, signed checks, signed photos, signed books and signed scraps must all be considered individually.

The following are prices for documents and signed 8x10 photograhs. The first price is for documents, the second for photos.

| | |
|---|---|
| Bud Abbott | 50-125 |
| Abbott & Costello | 100-300 |
| Pier Angeli | 25-60 |
| Susan B. Anthony | 75-150 |
| Roscoe "Fatty" Arbuckle | 75-300 |
| Louis Armstrong | 50-150 |
| Neil Armstrong | 25-50 |
| Fred Astaire | 20-50 |
| John J. Audubon | 100-0 |
| Theda Bara | 50-100 |
| L. Frank Baum | 125-0 |
| Irving Berlin | 30-125 |
| Humphrey Bogart | 75-300 |
| Napoleon Bonaparte | 200-0 |
| Clara Bow | 35-100 |
| Charles Boyer | 10-30 |
| Marlon Brando | 75-125 |
| Walter Brennan | 20-30 |
| Johnny Mack Brown | 10-30 |

---

## Only items in fine condition, please.

# Autographs

**Continued from previous page.** These prices are for documents and signed 8x10 photos. The first price is for documents, the second for photographs.

| | |
|---|---|
| Ethel Barrymore | 10-40 |
| John Barrymore | 50-125 |
| Lionel Barrymore | 10-40 |
| Beatles (all four) | 750-1250 |
| Alexander Graham Bell | 250-600 |
| Ingrid Bergman | 25-75 |
| Irving Berlin | 75-200 |
| William "Hopalong" Boyd | 40-100 |
| Burns and Allen | 35-100 |
| Richard Burton | 15-30 |
| Al Capone | 500-1,000 |
| Truman Capote | 25-75 |
| Cassius Clay | 50-150 |
| Walt Disney | 300-800 |
| Charles de Gaulle | 100-300 |
| Thomas Edison | 250-850 |
| William Faulkner | 200-400 |
| Clark Gable | 100-275 |
| Greta Garbo | 250-2,000 |
| Sigmund Freud | 600-1,500 |
| Judy Garland | 125-250 |
| Lou Gehrig | 200-600 |
| Cary Grant | 50-75 |
| Alexander Hamilton | 250-0 |
| Dashiell Hammett | 100-200 |
| David Janssan | 10-25 |
| Jacqueline Kennedy | 100-175 |
| John Kennedy | 450-2,000 |
| Robert Kennedy | 125-250 |
| Joseph Kennedy, Sr. | 75-150 |
| Martin Luther King, Jr. | 200-500 |
| Gypsy Rose Lee | 10-40 |
| Robert E. Lee | 750-0 |
| John Lennon | 200-300 |
| Sonny Liston | 75-125 |
| Joe Lewis | 50-200 |
| Bella Lugosi | 150-250 |
| Marilyn Monroe | 250-750 |
| Jim Morrison | 275-400 |
| Elvis Presley | 275-400 |
| George Reeves | 400-0 |
| Frederic Remington | 100-200 |
| Jack Ruby | 50-100 |
| Babe Ruth | 450-1,000 |
| Robert Louis Stevenson | 150-250 |

John Adams     500 -0

Thomas Jefferson     1,000-0

John Quincy Adams     150 -0

Abraham Lincoln     1,500-0

Ulysses S. Grant     175-0

Dwight Eisenhower     100-150

---

**Prices Paid by:**   Ivan Gilbert
Miran Arts & Books
2824 Elm Avenue
Columbus, OH 43209
(614) 818 3222 days     (614) 236-0002 nights     Fax (614) 818-3223

---

# Books & Autographs

We purchase books, autographs, manuscripts and related ephemera of important and lasting value, and are interested in individual titles and/or estate libraries of quality. Included are a few select examples from a number of subject areas. There are many variables in determining a book's intrinsic or extrinsic value (author, subject, edition, condition, binding, age, etc.), all of which are important to note when describing your book(s). Please indicate publisher and date from the title page. A photograph can be of assistance. A phone call is always welcome. (Please leave a detailed message if we are closed when you call.) These offers are for complete copies in good, original condition.

| Thomas. Golf Architecture. 1927 | 150 |
|---|---|
| Hammett. The Maltese Falcon. 1930 | 450 |

## AMERICANA

| | |
|---|---|
| Bourke. On the Border With Crook. 1891 | $125 |
| Johnson and Winter. Route Across the Rocky Mountains. Lafayette, 1846. | 1,250 |
| Lawson. New Voyage to Carolina. 1709. | 2500 |
| McKenney and Hall. Indians.1848-50. | 1,500 |
| Pike. Expeditions to the Mississippi. 1810 | 1,250 |

## ART & ARCHITECTURE

| | |
|---|---|
| Hunter. Papermaking By Hand. 1939 | $750 |
| Jones. Grammar of Ornament. 1856 | 175 |
| Peters. California on Stone. 1931 | 225 |
| Verve magazine (various issues) | 50-150 |
| Warhol. Andy Warhol's Index (Book). 1967 | 175 |

## CHILDREN'S BOOKS

| | |
|---|---|
| Baum. Mother Goose in Prose. 1897 | $750 |
| Baum. Wonderful Wizard of Oz. 1900 | 2,500 |
| Carroll. Alice's Adventures. 1869 | 350 |
| Dick and Jane titles, 1930s-1940s | 25-50 |
| Pyle. The Wonder Clock. 1888 | 75 |
| Early printed books, pre-1800 | 100 and up |

## ILLUSTRATED BOOKS

| | |
|---|---|
| Chagall. Illustrations for the Bible. 1956 | $1,750 |
| Nast. Christmas Drawings. 1890 | 125 |
| Saunders. The Knave of Hearts. 1925 | 250 |
| Ward, Lynd. God's Man.1929 | 150 |

## LIMITED EDITIONS

Books published in limited editions, usually far less than 1,000 cc, and especially printed on quality paper and binding, often signed.

| | |
|---|---|
| Aristophanes. Lysistrata. 1934 (LEC) | $1,250 |
| Grahame. Wind in the Willows. 1940 (LEC) | 250 |
| Joyce, James. Ulysses.1935 (LEC) | 1,750 |
| Steinbeck. Grapes of Wrath. 1940 (LEC) | 250 |
| Thoreau, H.D. Walden. 1936 (LEC) | 250 |

## LITERATURE

| | |
|---|---|
| Chandler, Raymond. The Big Sleep. 1939 | $1,250 |
| Dickinson, Emily. Poems. 1890 | 750 |
| Grafton, Sue. "A" is for Alibi.1982 | 250 |
| Hemingway. The Sun Also Rises. 1926 | 550 |
| James, Henry. The Ambassadors. 1903 | 75 |
| London. The Sea-Wolf. 1904 | 125 |
| Melville, Herman. Moby Dick. 1851 | 12,500 |
| Morris. Wood Beyond the World. 1894 | 450 |
| Nabokov. Lolita. 2 vols. 1955 | 325 |
| Salinger. Catcher in the Rye. 1951 | 500 |
| Steinbeck. Grapes of Wrath. 1939 | 375 |
| Tolkien, J.R.R. The Hobbit. 1937 | 650 |
| Twain. Celebrated Jumping Frog. 1867 | 750 |

## PHOTOGRAPHY

| | |
|---|---|
| Camera Work (magazine). 1903-17 | $250-500 |
| Cartier-Bresson. Decisive Moment. 1955 | 175 |
| Davidson. East 100th Street. 1970 | 75 |
| Frank, Robert. Americans. 1959 | 75 |
| Frith, Francis. Egypt and Palestine. 1859 | 1,500 |
| Klein, William. Tokyo / Paris. 1964 | 125 |
| Penn, Irving. Moments Preserved. 1960 | 150 |
| Original 19th century photographs | 25-250 |

## RELIGION & PHILOSOPHY

| | |
|---|---|
| Bibles, pre-1800 | $50 to 50,000 |
| Book of Common Prayer, pre-1700 | 150-500 |
| Glover. Science and Health. 1875 | 950 |
| Smith. Book of Mormon. 1830s-40s | 250-2,500 |

## SCIENCE & MEDICINE

| | |
|---|---|
| Babbage. Economy of Machinery. 1832 | $175 |
| Bell. Illustrations of Surgery. 1821 | 500 |
| Browne. Religio Medici. 1643 | 750 |
| Darwin. Journal of Researches. 1840 | 250 |
| Darwin. Origin of Species. 1859 | 2,500 |
| Lyell. Principles of Geology. 1833 | 350 |
| Osler. Principles of Medicine. 1892 | 250 |
| Tesla. Experiments Alt. Currents.1892 | 125 |
| Whitehurst. Inquiry into the Earth. 1778 | 225 |

## SIGNED BOOKS & AUTOGRAPHS

Please offer signed books and autograph material from all historical figure. No contemporary sports or Hollywood, please.

| | |
|---|---|
| Anthony, Susan B. signed letter | $200 |
| Austen, Jane. signed letter | 2,500 |
| Baum, L. Frank. signed letter | 250 |
| Boone, Daniel. signature | 800 |
| Brecht, Bertolt, signature | 125 |
| Bruckner, Anton. signed letter | 950 |
| Cather, Willa. A Lost Lady. 1923 | 250 |
| Cezanne, Paul. signed letter | 1,000 |
| Cline, Patsy. signature | 125 |
| Cody, William F. signed photograph | 500 |
| Cromwell, Oliver. signature | 500 |
| Custer, George A. signature | 1,250 |
| Darrow, Clarence. signed letter | 450 |
| Darwin, Charles. signed book | 350 |
| Davis, Jefferson. signed letter | 750 |
| Dickens, Charles. signed letter | 450 |
| Dickinson, Emily, signature | 175 |
| Disney, Walt. signature | 250 |
| Duncan, Isadora. signed photograph | 350 |
| Earhart, Amelia. signed photograph | 450 |
| Earp, Wyatt. signature | 1,250 |
| Einstein, Albert. signed photograph | 750 |
| Faulkner. Absalom, Absalom! 1936 | 550 |
| Ford, Henry. signed photograph | 750 |
| Foster, Stephen. signed letter | 1 500 |
| Franklin, Benjamin. signed letter | 3,750 |
| Gershwin, George. signed photograph | 1,500 |
| Grant, U.S. signature, as president | 375 |
| Hearn, Lafcadio. signed letter | 750 |
| Hooper, William.. signed letter | 600 |
| Homer, Winslow. autographed letter | 350 |
| Houdini, Harry. signed photograph | 750 |
| Jackson, Helen Hunt. autographed poem | 50 |

| | |
|---|---|
| James, Will. Smoky the Cowhorse. 1926 | 125 |
| Joyce, James, signed book | 250 |
| Kennedy, John F. autographed letter | 2,500 |
| King, Martin Luther, Jr. signature | 250 |
| Lee, Robert E. signature | 1250 |
| Lindbergh, Charles A. signature | 250 |
| Muir, John. signed letter | 650 |
| Oakley, Annie. signature | 450 |
| Parrish, Maxfield. signature | 50 |
| Pinchon, Thomas. signed letter | 750 |
| Quantrill, William C. signature | 250 |
| Rockefeller, John D. signed letter | 350 |
| Russell, Charles M. signed letter | 250 |
| Sutter, John A. signed letter | 1,500 |
| Salinger, J.D. signed letter | 750 |
| Stravinsky, Igor. signed photograph | 350 |
| Stuart, J. E. B. signature | 350 |
| Tesla, Nikola. signed letter | 475 |
| Twain, Mark. signed photograph | 1,750 |
| White, Ellen G. signed letter | 125 |
| Whitney, Eli. signature | 225 |
| Wright, Frank Lloyd. signed letter | 350 |
| Wyeth, Andrew. signature | 65 |

## TRAVEL & EXPLORATION

| | |
|---|---|
| Amundsen. The South Pole. 1912 | $125 |
| Atlases. United States, pre-1890 | 100-500 |
| Atlases. World, pre-1800 | 500-5,000 |
| Baedeker. United States. 1893 | 150 |
| Baedeker. Palestine and Syria.1876 | 150 |
| Burton, Richard. Sind Revisited. 1877 | 350 |
| Freshfield. Exploration of Caucusus. 1896 | 300 |
| Heriot. Travels Through the Canadas. 1807 | 750 |
| Mawson. Home of the Blizzard. 1915 | 225 |

| | |
|---|---|
| Mickey Mouse. pop-up books. 1933 | 175 |
| Morris. Wood Beyond the World. 1894 | 450 |

# Books & Catalogs

**TRADE CATALOGS** show goods and materials for sale. I try not to buy those issued after 1920. Standard Bibliographic format required.

| | |
|---|---|
| Khomiakoff, Moskovka, steam engine, London, 1851 | 50 |
| Amer. Road Machine. Illus. Cat., 1891, 32 pp., 5" x 8" | 25 |
| Fairbanks-Morse Home Water Service, 1934, 32 pp., 10" x 8" | 8 |
| Albany Cotton Gin circular, 1868, 24 pp., 10" x 8", edge gnawed | 20 |

**TUNE BOOKS WITH SHAPED NOTES** If unfamiliar, don't worry; see illustration. My interest is only for those printed prior to 1900, 5" or 6" high and 9" across. Don't be discouraged by the dates; I do buy later editions, proportionately priced.

| | |
|---|---|
| Boyd, J.S., *Virginia Sacred Musical*, 1816 | $200 |
| Carrell, *J.P., Songs of Zion*, 1810 | 200 |
| Clayton/Carrell, *Virginia Harmony*, 1831 | 150 |
| Davisson, *Kentucky Harmony*, 1816 | 150 |

Please request an author and title list.

### SHEET MUSIC... BOUND VOLUMES ONLY

These are usually 19th century and the price paid depends on the number and quality of the items bound in. Important to note any staining, tears, or repairs to pages. Helpful to note any illustrated covers (note if they are hand tinted). When describing, brief titles are fine.

| | |
|---|---|
| Telegraph Waltzes, c. 1847, 7p. | $12 |
| Old Rough and Ready Quick Step, 1846, 2p. | 8 |
| Welcome Home, 1848, 4p. | 5 |
| Perabeau, Honour to the Brave, 1846 | 15 |

**SPANISH AMERICAN WAR** All types of memorabilia, including proceedings of Sp/Am War Veterans Association. CAUTION: I'm buying for one customer, and you must allow time for me to write to and hear from him; then I can respond to you. This customer does not buy newspapers. Below are items already bought for him.

| | |
|---|---|
| Armstrong, *Pictorial Atlas Sp/Am War*, 1898 | $50 |
| White, *Our War With Spain* | 5 |
| *Santiago Campaign*, 1927 | 16 |
| *Sp/Am War by US War Dept*, 1899 | 13 |
| *Ditto. Vets. Ritual*, 1928 | 4 |

### CIVIL WAR AND 1ST PERSON NARRATIVES

Condition is important.

| | |
|---|---|
| Davis, *Rise and Fall/Confed. Govt.*, 2 vols. | $75 |
| Johnston, *Life/Albert Sidney johnston* | 35 |
| Jackson, *Life/Letters...Stonewall*, 1892 | 75 |
| Lee, *Memoirs Wm. Nelson Pendleton*, 1893 | 50 |

**SOUTHERN IMPRINTS/TITLES** Pre-1860. Please use Standard Bibliographic form. These are books printed in the south or about the South.

| | |
|---|---|
| Thomas, J., *White Pilgrim*, Winchester, VA, 1813 | $100 |
| Howison, *History of Virginia*, 2 vols. | 100 |
| *So. Lit. Messenger (Magazine)* per volume | 20-100 |

**APPALACHIAN AUTHORS** Customers believe dust jackets are so important, even though they constitute less than one percent of most books. But tell me about your book, even if it has no jacket.

| | |
|---|---|
| Post, M.D., Strange Schemes | $25 |
| Miles, Emma, Spirit of the Mountains | 50 |
| Simpson, Mountain Path | 50 |

**NEALE BOOKS (PUBLISHER)** Most have that name printed at the bottom of backstrip. CAUTION: many of the Neal bindings were vary attractive to insects, and the best way to describe them is to photocopy the covers and on the print darken in the flecked areas. Neale published nearly 100 Civil War titles and nearly 30 on Virginia.

| | |
|---|---|
| Anderson, *Fighting by So. Federals* | $35 |
| Ford, *Life in the Confederate Army* | 50 |
| O'Ferral, *Forty Years of Active Service* | 25 |
| Polley, *Soldier's Letters to Charming Nellie* | 200 |

**TECHNICAL BOOKS BEFORE 1920** Many of my customers love books about 19th or early 20th century grain mills, house building, weaving, optical instrumentation, carriages, coffins or cabooses. Most of these books were single topic (not a dictionary or general book); a book on the telegraph, for example, is of more interest than one on communication.

| | |
|---|---|
| Watson, *British... Building Btones*, 1911 | $18 |
| *Ruhmkoff induction Coils*, 1896 | 75 |
| Henry, *Elements of Exper. Chem.*, 1817 | 60 |
| Monteath, *new... System of Draining*, 1829 | 35 |
| Holtzapffel, *Turning and Mech. Manip.*, 6 vols. 1852+ | 250 |

*Notes are triangular, diamond, square & round.*

I appreciate your interest. If you want to know more about me, request my business bio.

**Prices Paid by:** Jim Presgraves, ABAA
Bookworm & Silverfish
P.O. Box 639
Wytheville, VA 24382

# Children's & Other Books

Series books come in two basic formats. Most series books copyright before 1960 should have a paper cover, called a dust jacket. Books printed after 1960 may come in a style called "pictorial cover." These books have a drawing in color on the front cover. The prices listed are for books in fine (as new) condition in like dust jackets. Pictorial cover books are noted p/c.

*This dust jacket is considered Very Good  $3*

| | | | |
|---|---|---|---|
| Nancy Drew | #s | 1-40 | $3-10 |
| depending on age and style of dust jacket | | | |
| Nancy Drew | p/c | | 1-1.50 |
| Judy Boltonp/c #s | | 30-38 | 5-100 |
| Hardy Boys | #s | 1-41 | 3-10 |
| with fine D.J. | | | |
| Cherry Ames | #s | 1-24 | 3-10 |
| Cherry Ames | #s | 25-27 | 5-20 |
| Chip Hilton | #s | 1-19 | 3-10 |
| Chip Hilton | #s | 20-23 | |
| p/c | | | 10-50 |
| Tom Swift, Sr. | #s | 1-40 | 3-10 |
| Tom Swift, Jr. | #s | 30-33 | |
| p/c | | | 10-20 |
| Rick Brant | #s | 20-24 | |
| p/c | | | 10-50 |
| Rick Brant | #s | 4-19 | 2-8 |

For most series with dust jackets, we will pay a minimum of $2 & postage. Please contact us for price quote. SASE appreciated.

If you have a more valuable book, we will tell you and pay accordingly.

## Encyclopedias

| | |
|---|---|
| Encyclopedia Judaica, 1972 | 125 |
| Inquire for other years | |
| Great books | |
| depending on binding | 75-100 |
| Inquire about World Book | |

We do not purchase The Book of Knowledge, Comptons, Colliers, supermarket sets, Household, Mother's, etc.

## Heritage Press

Must be fine (as new) condition, in original fine box, with Sandglass letter laid in. We buy most titles in lots as they are worth only $2-3 each. Some special ones are:

| | |
|---|---|
| Gone With The Wind, 2 vol. | $12 |
| Lewis and Clark, 2 vol. | 12 |
| Book of Ruth, Book of Job | each 6 |

## Limited Editions Club

Must be in fine (as new) condition, in original fine box.

| | |
|---|---|
| Lysistrata | 400 |
| Ulysses | 400 |
| Wind In The Willows | 150 |
| Voice of the City | 100 |
| Shakespeare 37 vols. | 250 |
| Through the Looking Glass | 150 |

Please call or write about other titles. There are over 500 titles.

We buy books in all fields except medicine and law. If you send SASE, we will help you sell your books, even if we can't use them, provided they have intrinsic value.

---

**Prices Paid by:**  Lee Temares
50 Heights Road
Plandome, NY 11030
(516) 627-8688  8am to midnite Eastern     Fax  (516) 627-7822

# Tobacco Collectibles

## CIGARETTE CARDS

I purchase cigarette insert cards for all brands of American cigarettes, especially color cards in complete sets issued by Duke, Kinney or Allen & Ginter. Complete sets are of greater interest than individual cards. The condition of cards is important and directly related to value. Prices quoted are for like new cards with sharp edges and corners and no creases. Some British cards are purchased but prices tend to be significantly less.

| | |
|---|---|
| A&G Celebrated Indian chiefs | $10 |
| A&G Generals | $10 |
| A&G Flags | .10 to $0.50 |
| A&G World's Smokers | $4 |
| D Breeds of Horses | $2.50 |
| D Histories of Generals | $10 |
| K Great American Trotters | $5 |
| K (photo style cards) | 0.50-$1.50 |
| Player & Sons Fishes (British) | .10 |
| Player & Sons Picturesque Bridges (British) | .75 |
| **Albums issued by U.S. companies** | **$40-$100+** |

## TOBACCO INSERT CARDS

I buy tobacco insert cards upon which the words cigars, plug, cut plug, navy, smoking, chewing, and the like appear. All cards considered, but premium prices are paid only for cards in like new condition.

| | |
|---|---|
| | $3-10 |
| Cigars (actresses) | $2+ |
| *Capadura* $1-$5 (most) $10-20 (political/baseball) | |
| *No-Tobac* | $5-10 |

## CIGARETTE SILKS

I purchase cigarette silks (actually made of satin) issued in more than 80 different sets, with flags the most common. Prices are for each undamaged item. Complete & clean sets add 15% to these prices.

| | |
|---|---|
| Flags | .10 |
| Large flags | .20 |
| Flags more than 8" | 2.00 |
| Automobile pennants | 5.00 |
| Baseball players | 6.00 |
| Butterflies | .25 |
| Generals | 5.00 |
| Girls (portrait in circle) | 3.00 |
| Indian portraits | 2.50 |
| large Indian portraits | 3.50 |
| King girls | 2.00 |
| Zira girls | 3.00 |

## CIGAR(ETTE) FELTS

I purchase cigar and cigarette felts (actually made of flannel) issued in more than 40 different sets with flags the most common. Prices are for each bright undamaged, clean item.

| | |
|---|---|
| Flags less than 8" long | .10 |
| Flags more than 12" long | $10 |
| Butterflies | .50 |
| Baseball players | $10-$30 |

## CIGAR(ETTE) LEATHERS

| | |
|---|---|
| Breeds of dogs | $1.00 |
| College pennants or seals | $0.50 |
| College fraternity seals | $1.00 |
| Indians (large pelt shaped leather) | $30 |

## CIGAR LABEL & OTHER CATALOGS

I buy all catalogs from cigar makers, pipe makers, tobacco companies, box makers, cigar label printers, leaf dealers, tobacco tools and all other tobacco products.

| | |
|---|---|
| Cigar label catalogs w/ paper covers | $100+ |
| Cigar label catalogs w/hard covers | $1,000+ |
| Cigar label catalogs FM Howell | $100-$200 |
| Coupon/premium catalogs | $5-$20 |
| Pictorial cigar catalogs showing factories | $30+ |

## TOBACCO TRADE DIRECTORIES

I pay $100 up for *Tobacco Trade Directories*, 1860 to 1940. I buy these hard cover state-by-state lists of cigar and tobacco manufacturers in any condition. Please call for an offer for any and all.

## PAPER EPHEMERA

I buy paper, bills, advertising flyers and/or letters with important or interesting content related to tobacco use, manufacture, buying or selling.

| | |
|---|---|
| US Tax regulations (cigar ) pre 1920 | $20+ |
| Report NYC Board of Health on tenements | $50 |
| Legal documents rel to tobacco 18th C | $10-50 |
| Legal documents rel to cigars 19th C | $10-50 |
| Anything related to cigars in US before 1800 | $30+ |

## PRINTS AND PHOTOS

I buy photos, prints and paintings showing tobacco being used, particularly cigar smokers. Also all prints or photos of cigar stores, cigar factories, tobacco salesmen, delivery wagons, etc. Photos and prints of US, Cuba and Canada preferred but some foreign are OK, especially related to the Amsterdam tobacco market.

| | |
|---|---|
| Paintings (unsigned) | $50-$200+ |
| Paintings (signed by unknowns) | $50-$200+ |
| Print "The Pig" being tied down (*Judge* c1908) | $75 |
| Print of Sam Gompers (*Leslies 1873*) | $50 |
| Photo of cigar factory exterior | $30+ |
| Photo of cigar factory interior | $40+ |
| Photo of cigar/tobacco delivery wagon | $50+ |

### HOW TO DESCRIBE WHAT YOU HAVE TO SELL

The best way to describe items is to make a Xerox™ whenever possible. Photos are also fine, if they are sharp and show detail. Make certain to describe condition accurately.

---

**Prices Paid by:** Tony Hyman
Box 3000-PG
Pismo Beach, CA 93448
(805) 773-6777    Fax (805) 773-8436
thyman@tobacciana.com

# NOTES

# NOTES